edexcel
advancing learning, changing lives

Edexcel GCSE
Religious Studies

Unit 1A
Religion and Life
Christianity
& Islam

Gordon Reid
Sarah Tyler

Published by Pearson Education Limited, a company incorporated in England and Wales, having its registered office at Edinburgh Gate, Harlow, Essex, CM20 2JE. Registered company number: 872828

www.heinemann.co.uk

Edexcel is a registered trade mark of Edexcel Limited

Text © Pearson Education Ltd 2009
First published 2009

13 12 11 10 09
10 9 8 7 6 5 4 3 2 1

British Library Cataloguing in Publication Data
A catalogue record for this book is available from the British Library.

ISBN 978 1 846904 19 6

Edited by Florence Production Ltd, Stoodleigh, Devon
Typeset by HL Studios, Long Hanborough, Oxford
Produced by Florence Production Ltd, Stoodleigh, Devon
Original illustrations © Pearson Education Ltd 2009
Illustrated by HL Studios, Long Hanborough, Oxford
Cover design by Pearson Education Ltd
Picture research by Zooid
Cover photo/illustration © blickwinkel/Alamy
Printed in the UK by Scotprint

Acknowledgements
The authors and publisher would like to thank the following individuals and organisations for permission to reproduce copyright material:

AFP/Getty Images/Ted Aljibe, p. 97; AFP/Getty Images/Joseph Barrak p. 53; AFP/Getty Images/Adek Berry, p. 65; AFP/Getty Images/Behrouz Mehri, p. 51; AFP/Getty Images/Kazuhiro Nogi, p. 22; akg-Images/Osri Battaglini, p. 32; Alamy/Ablestock, p. 18; Alamy/Peter Barritt, p. 4; Alamy/D. Burke, p. 77; Alamy/ClassicStock, p. 60; Alamy/Sally and Richard Greenhill, pp. 48, 72; Alamy/Glenn Harper, p. 32; Alamy/Mary Evans Picture Library, p. 39; Alamy/Robin Nelson, p. 11; Alamy/Marmaduke St. John, p. 105; Alamy/Shangara Singh, p. 44; Alamy/Homer Sykes/CountrySideCollection, p. 24; Alamy/Jack Sullivan, p. 12; Alamy/Jim West, pp. 2–3; AP/PA Photos/M. Lakshman, p. 81; BBC Photograph Library/BBC, p. 78, p. 109; Bridgeman Art Library/Bibliotheque Nationale/Archives Charmet, p. 34; Bridgeman Art Library/Vatican Museums and Galleries, pp. 30–31; Comstock Premium/Alamy/Jupiterimages, p. 89; Corbis UK Ltd, p. 70; Corbis UK Ltd/Bob Adelman, p. 98; Corbis UK Ltd/Bettmann, p. 36; Corbis UK Ltd/The Gallery Collection, p. 32; Corbis UK Ltd/Kaveh Kazemi, p. 69; Corbis UK Ltd/Mark M. Lawrence, p. 12; Corbis UK Ltd/So Hing-Keung, p. 32; Corbis UK Ltd/Les Stone Sygma, p. 42; Design Pics/Corbis/Don Hammond, p. 7; Epa/Corbis UK Ltd/Daniel Hambury, p. 74; Epa/Corbis UK Ltd/Manuel Lorenzo, p. 92; Epa/Corbis UK Ltd/Claudio Onorati, pp. 58–59; Everett/Rex Features/Newmarket, p. 90; Getty Images, p. 8; Getty Images/Scott Barbour, p. 103; Getty Images/Pressebildagentur, p. 99; Intuitivemedia, pp. 86–87; IStockphoto, p. 16; IStockphoto, p. 106; Library of Congress/Getty Images/Marion Trikosko, p. 101; Linographic, p. 15 Linographic, p. 16; PA Archive/PA Photos/Stefan Rousseau, p. 66; PA Photos/Dona Peters, p. 66; Photoshot/Carl De Souza, p. 107; Reuters/Corbis UK Ltd, p. 47; Reuters/Corbis UK Ltd/Kieran Doherty, p. 23; Reuters/Corbis UK Ltd/Luke Macgregor, p. 95; Reuters/Corbis UK Ltd/Ahmad Masood, p. 45 Reuters/Corbis UK Ltd/Stringer/India, p. 100; Rex Features/ITV, p. 108; Science Photo Library/Anatomical Travelogue, p. 40; Science Photo Library/Oscar Burriel, p. 9; Science Photo Library/NASA/ESA/STSCI/T. Rector, NRAO, p. 14; Shutterstock, p. 32; Amy Watts, p. 17. Photos in ExamZone: iStockphoto/Efendi Kocakafa, p.114; iStockphoto/Chris Schmidt, p.114; iStockphoto/Alex Slobodkin, p.114; iStockphoto/Stockphoto4u, p.120; iStockphoto/ZoneCreative, p.114.

Permissions acknowledgements
Scripture taken from the Holy Bible, New International Version®. Copyright © 1973, 1978, 1984 International Bible Society. Used by permission of Zondervan. All rights reserved.
About Islam and Muslims, p. 50; IPCI – Islamic Vision, Birmingham, UK, pp. 34, 35, 44, 45, 50, 51, 64, 65, 68, 73, 80, 93, 101.
Every effort has been made to contact copyright holders of material reproduced in this book. Any omissions will be rectified in subsequent printings if notice is given to the publishers.

The publisher would like to thank Christine Paul for her contributions.

Websites
There are links to relevant websites in this book. In order to ensure that the links are up to date, that the links work, and that the sites are not inadvertently linked to sites that could be considered offensive, we have made the links available on the Heinemann website at www.heinemann.co.uk/hotlinks. When you access the site, the express code is 4196P.

Disclaimer
This Edexcel publication offers high-quality support for the delivery of Edexcel qualifications.
Edexcel endorsement does not mean that this material is essential to achieve any Edexcel qualification, nor does it mean that this is the only suitable material available to support any Edexcel qualification. No endorsed material will be used verbatim in setting any Edexcel examination and any resource lists produced by Edexcel shall include this and other appropriate texts.

Copies of official specifications for all Edexcel qualifications may be found on the Edexcel website – www.edexcel.com

Contents

Welcome to this Edexcel GCSE in Religious Studies Resource

These resources have been written to support fully Edexcel's new specification for GCSE Religious Studies. Each Student Book covers one unit of the specification which makes up a Short Course qualification. Any two units from separate modules of the specification make up a Full Course qualification. Written by experienced examiners, and packed with exam tips and activities, these books include lots of engaging features to enthuse students and provide the range of support needed to make teaching and learning a success for all ability levels.

How to use this book

This book supports Module A Unit 1 Religion and Life, based on a study of Christianity and at least one, but not more than two, other religions. Because a large number of students choose to study Christianity and Islam, this book covers these two religions. However, please note that religions other than Islam can be studied for this exam.

This book is split into the four sections of the specification.

Features in this book

In each section you will find the following features:

- **an introductory spread** which introduces the topics and gives the Edexcel key terms and learning outcomes for the whole section

- **topic spreads** containing the following features:

  - **Learning outcomes** for the topic

  edexcel ⠿ key terms

  > **Specification key terms** – are emboldened and defined for easy reference

  ## Glossary

  Here we define other complex terms to help with understanding

- **Activities** and **For discussion** panels provide stimulating tasks for the classroom and homework

- a topic **Summary** captures the main learning points.

A dedicated suite of revision resources for complete exam success. We've broken down the six stages of revision to ensure that you are prepared every step of the way.

How to get into the perfect 'zone' for your revision.

Tips and advice on how to plan your revision effectively.

Revision activities and exam-style practice at the end of every section plus additional exam practice at the end of the book.

Last-minute advice for just before the exam.

An overview of what you will have to do in the exam, plus a chance to see what a real exam paper will look like.

What do you do after your exam? This section contains information on how to get your results and answers to frequently asked questions on what to do next.

ResultsPlus

These features are based on how students have performed in past exams. They are combined with expert advice and guidance from examiners to show you how to achieve better results.

There are five different types of ResultsPlus features throughout this book:

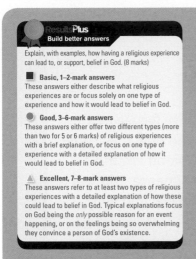

Build better answers: These give you an opportunity to answer some exam-style questions. They contain tips for what a basic ■ good ○ and excellent △ answer will contain.

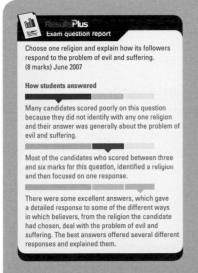

Exam question report: These show previous exam questions with details about how well students answered them.

■ Red shows the number of students who scored low marks (less than 35% of the total)

○ Orange shows the number of students who did okay (scoring between 35% and 70% of the total marks)

△ Green shows the number of students who did well (scoring over 70% of the total marks).

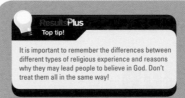

Top tip!: These provide examiner advice and guidance to help improve your results.

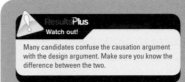

Watch out!: These warn you about common mistakes and misconceptions that examiners frequently see students make. Make sure that you don't repeat them!

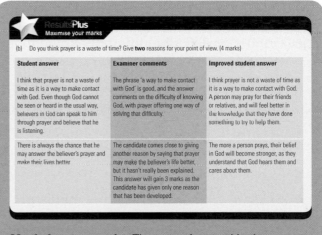

Maximise your marks: These are featured in the KnowZone at the end of each chapter. They include an exam-style question with a student answer, examiner comments and an improved answer so that you can see how to build a better response.

Believing in God

Introduction

This section is based on the study of one religion only. In this section we have focused on Christianity. In it, you will learn about what Christians believe about God and how they come to believe this, possibly through their upbringing, their appreciation of the world around them, or even through seeing a miracle take place or having a religious experience. You will also learn about how Christians deal with problems that challenge their beliefs; and why some people do not believe in God at all.

Learning outcomes for this section

By the end of this section you should be able to:

- Give definitions of the key words and use them in answers to GCSE questions
- Outline or describe the features of a Christian upbringing
- Explain how people come to believe in God through having a Christian upbringing, or a religious experience
- Outline or describe different explanations of the origins of the universe, including the 'causation', 'design' and scientific arguments
- Explain why scientific explanations of the origins of the universe cause some people to doubt God's existence, and how Christians respond to this
- Outline or describe other examples of problems which may cause some people to doubt God's existence; for example unanswered prayer, and evil and suffering
- Explain how Christians respond to these arguments
- Explain, with examples, how media programmes about religion may affect a person's attitude to belief in God
- Express with reasons and evidence your own opinion about the reasons for believing or not believing in God and other issues covered in this section.

edexcel ⁞⁞⁞ key terms

agnosticism	free will	natural evil	omnipotent
atheism	miracle	numinous	omniscient
conversion	moral evil	omni-benevolent	prayer

Young people deep in worship of God. Christian belief and practice are something that plays an active and relevant part in the lives of many young people today. It is important to remember this when studying this topic. Even if you find the idea of belief in God hard to understand, be open to thinking about why people do believe, not just to offering reasons why you think they shouldn't!

Fascinating fact

There are 34,000 different Christian groups or denominations in the world, and over 2,000 million individual Christians. Go to www.heinemann.co.uk/ hotlinks (express code 4196P) for more information on religious facts.

Take a sheet of A3 paper, turn it landscape, and write **GOD** in the middle of it. As a class, or in groups or pairs, create an ideas map focusing on words you think might describe God, attitudes believers and non-believers have towards God, and beliefs and practices associated with God. For example, you could start with **Father** (Christians speak of God as their Father), the **Bible** (believed to be the word of God), and **worship** (activities directed towards God to show him thanks and praise).

When you have finished studying this section you can turn back to this sheet and see if you want to add, change or take away any words.

1.1 Belief and non-belief in God

Learning outcomes

By the end of this lesson, you should be able to:

● understand and explain what it means to be a theist, atheist or agnostic

● describe what a theist believes

● explain reasons why an atheist rejects belief in God

● give your own opinions and the reasons for them.

edexcel ⠿ key terms

Agnosticism – Not being sure whether God exists.

Atheism – Believing that God does not exist.

Omni-benevolent – The belief that God is all-good.

Omnipotent – The belief that God is all-powerful.

Omniscient – The belief that God knows everything that has happened and everything that is going to happen

People have always tried to understand the ultimate questions in life. Questions such as 'Why are we here?', 'What happens when we die?', and 'Is there a God?'. The speech bubbles show different responses to these questions:

> Look at the world around us – it can't have happened by accident. It must have been designed by a greater intelligence – God, perhaps.

> When you die, you're just dead – there is no afterlife.

> We can't possibly know whether there is a God or not – there are some questions we just can't answer.

> If God exists, then why does he allow so many terrible things to happen?

> Lots of people claim to have experienced God in their lives. They can't all be wrong.

> There is no evidence that God exists. Science will soon be able to answer all the ultimate questions.

Someone who believes in God is called a theist. Someone who does not is called an **atheist.** A person who isn't sure and thinks it is impossible to know for certain if God exists or not is called an **agnostic**.

Glossary

Theist – A person who believes in God.

Activities

The famous ceiling of the Sistine Chapel.

Activities

1 Read the speech bubbles again.

(a) Decide for each one whether it is from a theist, an atheist or an agnostic; or whether you cannot tell.

(b) Which of the speech bubbles do you agree with? Give your reasons.

2 This is a famous picture by Michelangelo, showing God creating Man. Do you think it is realistic or not? Say why.

3 If God is all-powerful, is there anything he cannot do?

Can you list three possible things he could not do? To help, one might be that he cannot create a God greater than himself.

4

Christian beliefs about God

A Christian believes that:

- God created the world
- people can have a relationship with God
- he answers prayers and can perform miracles
- God is **omnipotent**, **omniscient** and **omni-benevolent.**
- belief in God gives meaning to life and helps people to answer difficult questions about death and suffering.

For discussion

Why do Christians think of God like this?

Atheists may have different reasons for not believing in God. Some atheists suggest that there is evidence that God does *not* exist, while others do not believe because, in their opinion, there is no evidence that he *does* exist.

Activities

4 Copy the spider diagram, then add some more legs to it so that you can add further reasons an atheist might have for not believing in God.

5 Draw another spider diagram for 'Arguments a theist might use for believing in God'.

Don't worry if you cannot think of many. You will find out about some more later in this section.

Other views

Agnostics will argue that, since there is no reliable evidence either in support of God's existence or against it, the only reasonable position to hold is literally 'not knowing'. An agnostic may argue that both the atheist and the theist have made a decision without sufficient evidence, and that agnosticism is the only approach we can take until there is more evidence for, or against, God's existence.

ResultsPlus
Watch out!

Some candidates confuse agnosticism with atheism – make sure that you know the difference between the two.

For discussion

- What are the main differences between an atheist and an agnostic?

Summary

- Theists believe in God and claim that everything is dependent on him for existence and meaning.
- Christians believe that God is omnipotent, omniscient and omni-benevolent.
- Atheists reject belief in God and claim that there is no evidence to support the claims theists make about God.
- Agnostics claim that there is not enough evidence to say whether God exists or not.

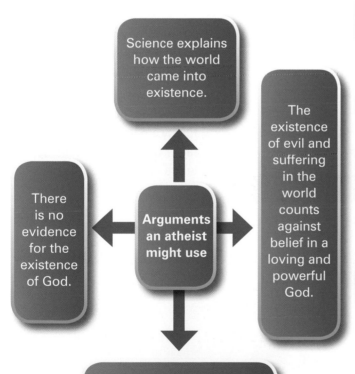

Science explains how the world came into existence.

There is no evidence for the existence of God.

Arguments an atheist might use

The existence of evil and suffering in the world counts against belief in a loving and powerful God.

Events and experiences that believers say are evidence for the existence of God are coincidences or natural events.

1.2 Religious upbringing

Learning outcomes

By the end of this lesson, you should be able to:

- describe ways in which Christian families encourage children to believe in God
- describe how religious communities contribute to a religious upbringing
- evaluate the importance of a religious upbringing in coming to believe in God
- give your own opinion on religious upbringing.

Glossary

Baptism – The Christian rite of initiation that welcomes a person into the Christian community.

Bible – The sacred text of Christianity.

Confirmation – Where a young Christian makes the baptismal vows for him- or herself.

Initiation ceremony – A ritual, such as baptism, which welcomes a person as a new member of a community or group that holds a certain set of beliefs.

Testimony – A public statement of faith and belief.

The role of parents

How you are brought up shapes the person you become. The way adults around you treat you, your experiences of the world you encounter, and the things you are told and introduced to all contribute to the person you become. This is known as your 'culture'. Think about your own childhood. Compare it to that of a young person growing up in America, Africa or India. What makes these young people different from you?

Many people come to believe in God through the way they are brought up. For Christians, one of the purposes of marriage is to have children and to bring them up in a secure Christian home. Christian parents introduce their children to belief in God and encourage their children to develop a relationship with God because they believe that this is the way God intended us to live and that it gives meaning and purpose to life. Some of the ways in which Christian parents create a religious upbringing are shown on the next page.

For discussion

- Do you think parents should encourage their children to follow a particular religious faith? Or should children be left to make up their own minds about religion and God?
- Should children always obey their parents?

Activities

1 Make a list of the different ways in which parents can encourage their children to believe in God. What, in your opinion, are the most effective ways?

2 Describe some of the problems that being raised in their parents' religion could bring as children grow older.

Sometimes, as they grow up, it is difficult for children to continue to accept their family's religious beliefs. The children will learn about other beliefs and ways of life and, at some point, will need to work out for themselves if what they have learned while growing up will be right for them in the future. This can be difficult for parents to understand. For other children, the comfort of growing up in a religious home can help them through difficulties and give them a secure basis for adulthood.

Baptism
During baptism, the child is welcomed into the Church, the family of God. Godparents, friends and the congregation promise to bring up the infant in the Christian faith and to be a good Christian example to the developing child.

Worship
The young child is taken to church on a regular basis. They are taught stories in Sunday School about Jesus, God and the Church. The majority of the people the young child meets believe in God and they all encourage the developing faith. The most memorable events in the young person's life will be the special occasions celebrated; these will usually be Christian festivals such as Christmas or Easter.

Adulthood
As the child grows into an adult, their Christian beliefs stay with them and are an integral part of their memories of happy, secure times. Should difficulties arise, the Christian community will be supportive through actions and prayer. It is from within the community in which they are established that they are likely to meet and marry someone who shares their beliefs. Once married, they have children and believe that a Christian upbringing offers children stability. They repeat the process and pass on their faith and beliefs. In the Bible it says, 'Bring a child up in the way he should go and he will not depart from it'.

A family at prayer.

School
Christian parents will often choose a Church school as this continues to surround their child with a strong sense of a community that all believe the same thing.

Confirmation
Christian parents, the Church and Church schools will all encourage children to make a commitment to their faith. This is known as confirmation and is when children confirm for themselves the vows their parents made for them when they were baptised.

Being part of the community
Churches often provide social events that bring the community and the family together. These may be prayer meetings, Bible study groups or purely social events such as youth clubs and parties to celebrate festivals. This sense of belonging helps the young person to express their faith and build friendships with other people of their own age who believe in the same things.

Activities

3 Outline the features of a Christian upbringing in your own words.

4 Explain how a Christian upbringing might lead to or support belief in God.

For discussion

- 'Parents should not force their religion on to their children.' Do you agree?

- How might Christian parents who attend church and believe in God avoid bringing up their children to believe in the same things as themselves? Is this possible?

- What other things might influence a person as they get older? Would these things affect their belief in God?

Summary

- Parents help children to believe in God by bringing them up in a religious family.

- Parents and their children may share beliefs, practices and activities together and with their religious community.

- Children will need to make their own choices about what they believe when they are older.

1.3 Religious experience (1)

Learning outcomes

By the end of this lesson, you should be able to:

- describe different types of religious experience
- explain the nature of religious experience
- explain why a religious experience may lead to, or support, belief in God
- evaluate different people's and your own beliefs about religious experiences.

Activities

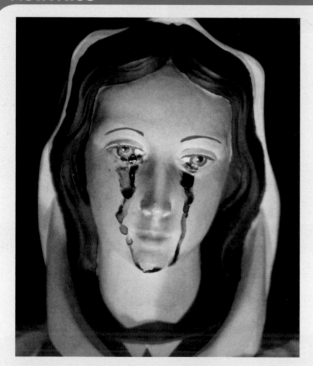

What can you see in this picture?

1 The picture shows a statue of the Virgin Mary weeping. Using this example, explain how miracles could help people to believe in God.

2 Do you think that people can really hear God's voice or see visions? Give reasons for and against your views.

edexcel ⠿ key terms

Miracle – Something that seems to break a law of science and makes you think only God could have done it.

Glossary

Holiness – Having the characteristic of being set apart for God's purposes.

Mystical experience – Experiencing God's voice or a religious vision.

Near-death experience – An experience after clinical death and before resuscitation.

In today's world many people come to faith in God following a religious experience that has convinced them that God exists. Such experiences include:

- seeing a religious vision
- witnessing a miracle
- having their prayers answered
- just a feeling of the presence of God near them (numinous)
- having a life-changing experience which leads them to commit themselves to God (conversion).

Many people claim to have had a religious experience – some studies suggest it may be as many as 75 per cent of the population. They need not be dramatic experiences, but might be an answered prayer or simply the feeling of God being with them, but such an experience can make a significant difference to how a person views the world and may change their life in an important way.

For discussion

Do you think that God really communicates with people? If so, what are the ways God communicates?

What is a miracle?

Many people claim to have experienced a **miracle** in their lives. A miracle is an act of God that goes against the laws of nature and is performed for a religious reason. An example would be the statue weeping shown on page 8 or a person making a full recovery after doctors had diagnosed their illness as terminal.

The New Testament teaches that Jesus performed miracles during his ministry, in order to make known who he was and to illustrate his teaching. He is recorded as curing the sick, calming storms, feeding crowds with very little food, and even raising the dead back to life.

- Mark 5:35–41 (the calming of the storm)
- Luke 8:40–56 (the healing of Jairus's daughter and the woman with the haemorrhage)
- Matthew 14:13–21 (the feeding of the 5,000)
- John 11:1–44 (the raising of Lazarus)
- Acts 3:1–10 (the healing of the crippled man)

Activities

Select any three stories from the list of biblical stories above.

3 (a) Write down the titles of the stories you have chosen.

(b) Then for each one write down whether you think it was a miracle or not. If you don't think it was a miracle, write down what you think actually happened.

4 Do you think any of the stories are particularly convincing? Give your reasons.

Mystical experiences include hearing God's voice or seeing a vision, possibly of Jesus or other religious figure or symbol. In the Old Testament, Isaiah had a mystical experience when he saw the throne of God and heard the angels wondering who would be a messenger for God. Isaiah was overwhelmed by the holiness of this experience, saying: '*Woe is me! For I am lost; for I am a man of unclean lips, and I dwell in the midst of a people of unclean lips; for my eyes have seen the King, the Lord of hosts*' (Isaiah 6:5).

Activities

5 Describe two different types of religious experience. See if you can find some recent examples on the Internet.

6 Explain how having a religious experience might lead someone to believe in God.

Other people have had a near-death experience, sometimes during an operation or when they lose consciousness after an accident. Although they are resuscitated (brought back to life by doctors), they believe that before this they have visited the afterlife, sometimes meeting a religious figure, passing through a tunnel of light, and perhaps given a review of their life. Not everyone agrees that these are religious experiences but, for some people, these events convince them to reconsider how they have lived their life and to commit themselves and their future to God.

An impression of what a near-death experience is like.

For discussion

Do you think that near-death experiences are real? If not, how could they be explained?

ResultsPlus
Top tip!

It is important to remember the differences between different types of religious experience and reasons why they may lead people to believe in God. Don't treat them all in the same way!

1.4 Religious experience (2)

Conversion

Some believers have **conversion** experiences, during which their beliefs change from one faith to another, or from no faith to believing in God. Conversion experiences can be dramatic. One of the best-known accounts is that of Saul, a learned Jew, who opposed the early Christians. His experience is described in Acts 9:4–5:

'As he neared Damascus on his journey, suddenly a light from heaven flashed around him. He fell to the ground and heard a voice say to him, "Saul, Saul, why do you persecute me?"

"Who are you, Lord?" Saul asked.

"I am Jesus, whom you are persecuting," he replied.'

God made him blind for three days during which time he came to a lasting faith in Jesus.

Some conversion experiences are much gentler, and come after years of quiet searching for a relationship with God.

Numinous experiences

A **numinous** experience is when something completely astonishes you. It is such an experience that words are not enough to describe the feeling, but it leaves you knowing that there must be something more powerful than you.

Often, people refer to things in the natural world that are so beautiful they feel overwhelmed by them – for example, the view from a mountain top or a beautiful sunrise. For others it may be an experience such as the birth of a baby. For some people this experience is so powerful that it convinces them that God must exist.

Prayer

Prayer is another kind of religious experience and is the way in which religious believers communicate with God through words or silent meditation. Prayer offers a means of drawing closer into a real and loving relationship with God and is a vital part of Christian belief and practice.

edexcel ::: key terms

Conversion – When your life is changed by giving yourself to God.

Numinous – The feeling of the presence of something greater than you.

Prayer – An attempt to contact God, usually through words.

Glossary

Confession of sins – Admitting wrongdoing against God.

Intercession – Praying for others.

Meditation – Thinking deeply about spiritual things.

Petitions – Requests made of God.

Thanksgiving – Giving thanks to God for what God has done.

Worship – Praising God.

The more a Christian prays, the more they will become convinced of the reality of God as a Father who hears them and cares about them. Christians share their hope and fears with God, as well as giving him thanks for the things he has done in their lives. Jesus prayed often and taught his disciples to do likewise, offering them the Lord's Prayer as a model to follow.

Different types of prayer

- Praising God through worship
- Praying for the needs of others through intercession
- Showing gratitude through thanksgiving
- Asking God for forgiveness through confession of sins
- Asking God to meet your own needs through petitions.

Jesus also taught:

'Ask and it will be given to you; seek and you will find; knock and the door will be opened to you. For everyone who asks receives; he who seeks finds; and to him who knocks the door will be opened.' (Matthew 7:7–8)

A Christian may pray alone or with a group. Many Christian prayers are formal and liturgical (read from a written form of service). However, other Christians prefer to pray spontaneously, devising prayers to meet particular needs. Some believers meditate quietly, focusing their thoughts on the nature of God, on a verse from scripture, or on listening in order to hear God's voice.

Christians praying during worship.

Activities

1 Do you think God answers prayers today? Give your reasons why or why not.

2 Choose one of the forms of prayer and write a prayer of this type.

3 How might prayer support a person's belief in God?

ResultsPlus
Build better answers

Explain, with examples, how having a religious experience can lead to, or support, belief in God. (8 marks)

■ **Basic, 1–2-mark answers**
These answers either describe what religious experiences are or focus solely on one type of experience and how it would lead to belief in God.

● **Good, 3–6-mark answers**
These answers either offer two different types (more than two for 5 or 6 marks) of religious experiences with a brief explanation, or focus on one type of experience with a detailed explanation of how it would lead to belief in God.

▲ **Excellent, 7–8-mark answers**
These answers refer to at least two types of religious experiences with a detailed explanation of how these could lead to belief in God. Typical explanations focus on God being the *only* possible reason for an event happening, or on the feelings being so overwhelming they convince a person of God's existence.

Summary

- Some people come to believe in God through a religious experience.
- Religious experiences include miracles, conversions, numinous experiences and communicating with God through prayer.

1.5 The design argument

Learning outcomes

By the end of this lesson, you should be able to:

● explain the design argument for the existence of God

● evaluate the design argument and give your own opinions about it.

Glossary

Analogy – A way of comparing two similar things to highlight their similarities.

Design – The appearance of order and purpose.

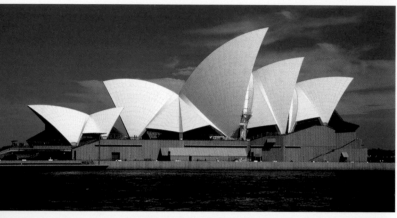

Examples of things that have been designed.

People have always had to design things – that is, to rearrange and change things in order to make them useful, functional or beautiful. For example, on the left, we have the Sydney Opera House and a space rocket. These structures did not come about by accident – they were designed.

Many people believe that the world, and the universe, were designed. They did not come about just by accident but were designed and made by God.

They believe God designed the world because:

● The world appears to be well ordered (for example, the laws of science such as gravity)
● The world is beautiful
● The things in the world appear to have a purpose for which they were designed (for example, animals and plants are suited to where they live)
● All the parts had to be put together in the right way for them to fulfil that purpose.

How do we know if the world is designed?

The scientist Isaac Newton was convinced of the existence of a 'designer' by looking at his thumbprint. Because all people have a unique thumbprint, he argued that this was evidence of the existence of a 'designer God'.

The beauty of the world doesn't, in itself, seem to serve any practical purpose and this could also suggest a loving God who wants to make things attractive for his creation.

However, this argument depends on accepting that the world and the universe *are* beautiful and orderly. Some people argue that they are ugly and chaotic, and therefore we cannot necessarily use this as an argument for God's existence.

Overview of the design argument

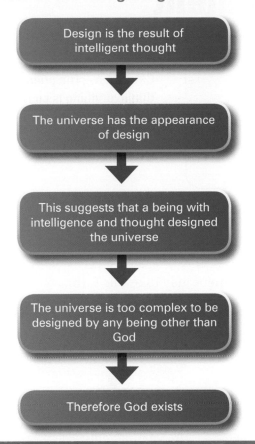

Design is the result of intelligent thought

↓

The universe has the appearance of design

↓

This suggests that a being with intelligence and thought designed the universe

↓

The universe is too complex to be designed by any being other than God

↓

Therefore God exists

Activities

1 List some examples from the natural world that appear to have been 'designed'.

2 **(a)** List all the facts in support of the design argument, then list all those against.

 (b) Which list, in your view, contains the most convincing arguments, and why?

3 If you were God, would you have designed the world differently? What changes would you have made?

4 'The design argument fails to provide convincing proof of the existence of God.' Do you agree? Give your reasons.

Paley's watch

The design argument uses a series of observations about the world that lead to the conclusion that God exists.

Watch out!

Many candidates confuse the causation argument with the design argument. Make sure you know the difference between the two.

A famous philosopher, William Paley, made an analogy between the watch and the world, both of which have complex and distinctive features. He said that if someone found a watch (an old-fashioned watch with cogs and wheels inside) and had never seen one before in their life, they would be curious and amazed. They would naturally assume that something that was so carefully made, and that was so dependent on all the correct pieces being in the right place at the right time, must have been designed and created by a very clever person. Paley argued that the same could be said of the universe, which is much more complicated. It could never have happened by chance; it must have had a clever designer and powerful creator. The only possible being capable of this is God. Therefore, he concluded, God exists.

Summary

- Some Christians argue that the appearance of the world supports belief in God.
- The design argument is based on the principle that the world is so orderly and purposeful that it cannot have come about by chance, but is rather the work of a designing God.

1.6 The causation argument

Learning outcomes

By the end of this lesson, you should be able to:

- explain the argument for the existence of God based on causation
- evaluate the causation argument and give your own opinions about it.

Glossary

Causation – The principle that everything is caused by something else.

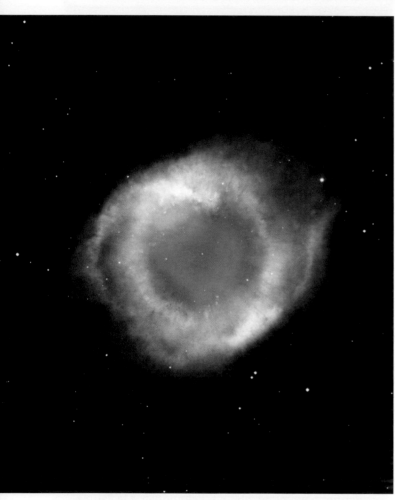

The Helix Nebula, sometimes called 'the Eye of God'. Do you think that the Nebula just happened naturally, or did God cause it to happen? Say why.

Things don't happen by chance!

There seems to be an accepted understanding that when things happen something or someone must have caused them. Some people use this idea to explain the existence of the universe.

They argue that nothing happens by chance – everything has a reason or a cause. This argument is known as causation.

The argument may take this form.

Overview of the causation argument

Nothing can happen by itself

↓

Everything that happens must be caused by something else

↓

The universe cannot have happened by itself

↓

A very powerful cause was necessary to bring the universe into being

↓

This cause has to be God

↓

Therefore, God exists.

Activities

1 Make a list of five things (for example, an apple or a book), and show how each one was *caused* to come into being. Is there anything in nature that is *not* caused?

The unmoved mover

The causation argument is also known as the cosmological argument. It is associated with the medieval Christian thinker Thomas Aquinas. He wrote:

> 'In the cosmos as we experience it, it is obvious to us that some things change. Now, whatever changes must be changed by another. And if that other itself changes then that too must be changed by another. But this cannot go on to infinity… You eventually have to arrive at something that is unchanging. This is God.'
> (Summa Theologica)

What Aquinas means is that eventually there has to be something which is the unmoved mover or first cause, and this has to be God.

Activities

2 Look at the picture of a rose. Do you think it was caused? Give your reasons.

Activities

3 How might the causation argument lead people to belief in God? Discuss with a partner and then write a short paragraph explaining the argument.

4 In groups, prepare a short presentation to the class on the design argument and the causation argument. Remember to include:
   - an overview of the arguments
   - reasons why they might lead people into believing in God
   - criticisms of the arguments.

Criticism of the causation argument

These arguments are often criticised by non-believers on the grounds that they make claims we cannot possibly prove to be true. Just because everything in our world seems to have a cause does not mean that the universe had to have a cause.

Critics of the argument might also argue that, even if there is a cause, that cause is not necessarily God. Or, if everything has a cause, then what 'caused' God?

For discussion

- What are the strengths and weaknesses of the causation argument? Which are the most convincing and why?
- Which is the stronger argument – design or causation? Why?

Summary

- The causation argument is based on the principle that nothing causes itself and it must therefore be caused by God.

1.7 Scientific explanations of, and Christian responses to, the origins of the world

Learning outcomes

By the end of this lesson, you should be able to:

- describe some scientific explanations of the origins of the world
- explain why some people do not believe in God because they feel that science offers a better explanation of the origin of the world
- express your own opinions about scientific explanations of the origins of the world
- outline different Christian responses to scientific explanations of the origins of the world.

Glossary

'Big bang' theory – The theory that an enormous explosion started the universe around 15 billion years ago.

Creationists – Religious believers who believe that the world was created by God in six days, exactly as described in Genesis.

Evolution – The gradual development of species over millions of years.

Natural selection – The way in which species naturally select the best characteristics for survival.

According to Darwin, modern dogs have evolved over the centuries from wolf-like creatures.

For people who do not believe in God there appear to be other explanations about how the world began (its origins). One of the most popular scientific theories is the 'big bang'. In its simplest form, this is the idea that an explosion of matter took place about 15 billion years ago and, from this explosion, the universe came into being and it continues to expand and evolve without any involvement from an outside power.

Charles Darwin, after studying animals and insect life from different countries, came to the conclusion that all living things had evolved over a period of time to suit the environment in which they found themselves. Each generation of animals therefore improved and evolved to survive. According to modern scientists, apes have common genetic material with human beings, and this indicates that humans evolved from apes. Darwin's theory suggests that God did not create all life uniquely but, rather, it evolved from one source.

Activities

1 Outline the scientific explanation for the origins of the universe.

2 Explain why this may cause some people to doubt God's existence.

3 'Animals still evolve and adapt to their environments. This proves that God did not create them.' Do you agree? Give reasons for your answer.

One of the key reasons that these theories lead people to doubt God's existence is because they are supported by evidence that can be seen and tested. For example, fossils have been found that show the development of some animals into more complex forms. Scientists acknowledge that, at the moment, theories about the origin of the world cannot be totally explained by science but claim that they will be in the future.

Activities

4 One person who supports Darwin's theory is the atheist Richard Dawkins. Look up his work and ideas on the computer and write a short explanation of why he does not believe in God. He uses the phrase 'purpose coloured spectacles'. What do you think this means?

Christian responses to scientific explanations of the world

Some Christians believe that these scientific theories are totally compatible with believing in God. They would argue that the 'big bang' and evolution do not prove that God does not exist – in fact, they would say that they were part of God's plan and God has used the process of evolution to create life.

These Christians believe that the Bible's description of the creation of the world in Genesis is not literally true. They believe that the Bible should be interpreted and that the message and the meaning is truth but some of the stories in the Bible are not actually what happened. They accept that science tells us *how* the world came into being but the Bible tells us *why* it came into being. They would say that the 'six days' in which God created the world are symbolic stages in the process of creation, not actual periods of time.

For discussion

- What is the most important question? How did we get here? Or why are we here?

However, not all Christians agree with this. Some Christians believe that the only way to respond to scientific explanations of the world is to reject them as false. They argue that the account of creation in Genesis is the literal truth. These Christians are called creationists. They believe that the world was created by an omnipotent God in six days.

Activities

5 What is the message being put over in the picture? Is it pro- or anti-creationist?

6 'Science will never succeed in disproving the existence of God.' Do you agree? Write a short paragraph giving reasons for your answer.

Summary

- Many atheists do not believe in God because they believe that science explains the creation of the world without the need for a God.
- Some Christians accept these scientific explanations, believing that they do not disprove the existence of God.
- Other Christians reject scientific explanations and believe in the literal truth of the Bible.

1.8 Unanswered prayers

Learning outcomes

By the end of this lesson, you should be able to:

- describe the problem of unanswered prayers
- explain why unanswered prayers are a problem for religious believers
- describe some Christian responses to the problem of unanswered prayers
- give your own opinions on unanswered prayers.

You have already looked at prayer and the way in which it helps people to feel closer to God (see pages 10–11). If people's prayers are answered then their belief in God will be strengthened. However, sometimes people's prayers are not answered. There are many people who have experienced suffering and pain in their own lives or witnessed these in the lives of others, and who have prayed to God, but feel that their prayers have not been answered. This may lead them to question their belief in God, or to reject him, or to believe that he does not exist.

From an early age, Christians are taught to pray to God.

An atheist may feel that if a loving God existed, then he would surely answer prayers. Many people experience suffering and pain in their own lives and see them in the lives of their family and friends, and when God seems to do nothing about it, it may be easy to reject belief in him. For some atheists, the suffering in the world, even when it doesn't affect them personally, persuades them that there is no God, especially when people praying all over the world seems to make no difference.

Activities

1 Explain in your own words why unanswered prayers may lead people to doubt God's existence.

2 Do you think that God answers prayers? Explain your reasons.

For discussion

How do you think a religious believer would feel if God did not answer their prayers?

Christian responses to unanswered prayers

Christians sometimes experience their prayers not being answered in the way they were hoping or expecting, and sometimes they don't seem to be answered at all. This can be a challenge to their faith. For some, this may mean that they turn away from God. Others accept that although God hears and answers prayer, he does not always answer in the way that they hope he will. Sometimes God's answer to a request is 'no'. This is hard for believers to accept, but they will try to understand God's answer and grow closer in their relationship with him.

Others, however, believe that God is answering prayers, but perhaps not in the way they expected. Or, some believe, it is because what they are praying for is not part of God's will or God's plan. Christians believe that God is not just there to grant whatever prayers a Christian asks. Instead, he grants the prayers that help to fulfil his divine plan for the world. They would say that people cannot possibly understand the mind of God.

Activities

3 Give three examples of prayers that God might say 'no' to.

4 'God doesn't care about our individual needs.' Do you agree? Give your reasons.

ResultsPlus
Build better answers

'Unanswered prayers prove that God does not exist.' In your answer you should refer to at least one religion.

(i) Do you agree? Give reasons for your opinion. (3 marks)

■ **Basic, 1-mark answers**

These answers offer a simple comment giving a person's own opinion.

● **Good, 2-mark answers**

Answers that receive 2 marks either offer two reasons for their views or one reason with a detailed explanation.

▲ **Excellent, 3-mark answers**

The best answers give at least two reasons with detailed explanations. They need to respond to what some religious believers would say. For example, 'Many Christians would say that… but I disagree with this because…'.

(ii) Give reasons why some people will disagree with you. (3 marks)

■ **Basic, 1-mark answers**

These answers would offer a simple opinion with a reason.

● **Good, 2-mark answers**

These answers either offer one reason that is well-explained or two simple reasons.

▲ **Excellent, 3-mark answers**

The best answers would either give three simple reasons, or two reasons with some explanation or evidence, or a fully-developed explanation of how the reasons support the opinion.

Praying effectively

Possibly an answer to offering prayers that God will be able to respond to positively is to concentrate on praying for God's will to be done rather than making specific requests to him. Some Christians pray in tongues so that they leave the precise content of the prayer to the Holy Spirit. Some may simply say the Lord's Prayer when they don't know what to ask of God. It is fair to say that God cannot say 'yes' in agreement to a prayer that is selfish or something that is against his will. For example, God might answer 'not yet' to a prayer for a car, but would answer 'no' to 'please make my teacher ill'. It seems likely that he would answer 'yes' to 'Please help all those who are suffering', although he could not do so by wiping out all suffering straight away. To the prayer 'Please let Fulham F.C. win the premier league', he would probably answer 'That's up to them to play well enough!'.

Summary

- Many people use unanswered prayers as a reason for not believing in God.

- Some Christians believe that some prayers are unanswered because they do not fulfil God's plan.

1.9 The problem of evil and suffering

Learning outcomes

By the end of this lesson, you should be able to:

- describe the problem of evil and suffering
- explain why evil and suffering is a problem for religious believers

edexcel ⠿ key terms

Moral evil – Actions performed by humans that cause suffering.

Natural evil – Things that cause suffering but have nothing to do with humans.

Evil can be understood as wickedness (the worst kind of badness or nastiness), which causes people to suffer pain and sorrow, both physical and non physical. Even though we all experience many good things in life, we cannot deny the existence of evil and suffering: war, terrorism, poverty, crime, sickness and unhappiness of all kinds are around us all the time. Sometimes we are forced to face massive events that cause suffering of the worst kind – for example, the Holocaust, the attack on the Twin Towers in 2001, or the tsunami which affected several countries in Asia in December 2004.

People also experience personal suffering, which sometimes we know nothing about, as they go through bereavement, illness, rejection, depression and loss.

For discussion

'Killing people is always evil and wrong.'
Do you agree?

There are two main types of evil and suffering:

- **Moral evil** – evil actions deliberately carried out by people that bring suffering to others, e.g. murder, rape, war, theft.
- **Natural evil** – suffering beyond people's control, caused by nature, e.g. famine, disease, natural disasters

Sometimes these two types of evil overlap, or they simply do not fit these categories. In fact, it might be hard to decide whether they are evil.

War (a moral evil) may lead to famine because the agricultural system breaks down (a natural evil); or cancer (a natural illness) can be caused by smoking or poor diet, which is an individual choice, so is it actually a moral evil? Is death an evil? If people never died would that be worse than death? How should we feel about animal suffering? If animals are abused by people, that must be a moral evil, but what about the suffering of an animal killed by a lion?

Not all suffering is caused by evil. Sometimes people make personal choices, such as taking dangerous drugs, which lead to suffering. In these cases can we be clear about who, if anyone, is to blame for that suffering?

Activities

1 Write a list of 10 'evil' things and divide them into moral and natural evil. With a partner choose the 5 most evil things in your lists. Put these in order: starting with 'the most evil is…' and finishing with 'the least evil is…' Discuss these as you do it and give reasons for each of your decisions. What makes something more evil than someting else?

2 Have a look at one of today's newspapers and make a list of all the news stories involving suffering.

(a) Identify those that are about moral evil and those that are about natural evil. Some may be a mixture of both.

(b) Say what caused each incident and how it might have been prevented.

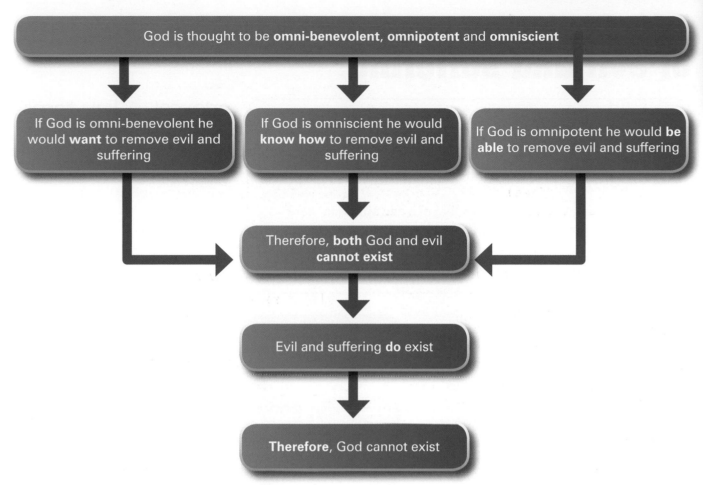

God is thought to be **omni-benevolent, omnipotent** and **omniscient**

If God is omni-benevolent he would **want** to remove evil and suffering

If God is omniscient he would **know how** to remove evil and suffering

If God is omnipotent he would **be able** to remove evil and suffering

Therefore, **both** God and evil **cannot exist**

Evil and suffering **do** exist

Therefore, God cannot exist

The existence of evil and suffering is often said to be one of the strongest arguments against the existence of God. This is known as the problem of evil and it can be outlined as shown on page 21:

This is a powerful argument as it questions both the existence and the characteristics of God.

In other words, if the existence of evil and suffering counts against God's love and power, then does he exist at all? Some believers may suggest that God does not, after all, need to be both all-loving and all-powerful.

However, for most believers these are not satisfactory solutions and they need to find a way to solve the problem without denying the existence of God or the existence of suffering.

Activities

3 **(a)** Does evil always lead to suffering?

   (b) Is suffering always wrong?

   Explain your answers to these questions.

4 Imagine you are having a conversation with God.

   (a) What questions would you ask God about the problem of evil and suffering?

   (b) What answers do you think God would give? Why?

Summary

Evil and suffering occur in many forms and can pose significant problems for those who believe in an all-loving, all-powerful and all-knowing God.

1.10 Christian responses to the problem of evil and suffering

Learning outcomes

By the end of this lesson, you should be able to:

- describe ways in which Christians attempt to solve the problem of evil and suffering
- explain how the Bible teaches that evil and suffering were brought into the world through people's sinfulness
- give your own opinions about the problem of evil and whether or not it disproves the existence of God.

edexcel ⠿ **key terms**

Free will – The idea that human beings are free to make their own choices.

The problem of evil and suffering can pose the biggest challenge to belief in God for some Christians.

Chapters 1 to 3 of Genesis describe how God created the world and people, and suggest that in the beginning the world was perfect. However, Adam and Eve disobeyed God and, as a result, evil and suffering entered the world and they, Adam and Eve, were separated from God.

'*So the Lord God banished him [Adam] from the garden of Eden to work the ground from which he had been taken.*' (Genesis 3:23)

The positive outcome of this account in Genesis doesn't come until the New Testament. Christians believe that God sent his son, Jesus, to overcome the evil that had come into the world because of the events that took place in the Garden of Eden. Because Jesus was the sinless Son of God, he could take the punishment for all of humankind's sins, dying in their place. If people believe in Jesus and what he achieved on the cross, they will be forgiven for their sin and can look forward to eternity with God.

'*For God so loved the world that he gave his one and only Son, that whoever believes in him shall not perish but have eternal life.*' (John 3:16)

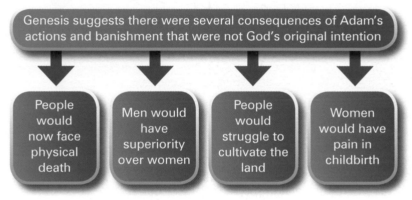

Genesis suggests there were several consequences of Adam's actions and banishment that were not God's original intention

| People would now face physical death | Men would have superiority over women | People would struggle to cultivate the land | Women would have pain in childbirth |

A test from God?

Some Christians believe that evil and suffering is a test from God. God allows believers to go through difficult times in order to see how they will react to them. For example, some believers may grow closer to God and become stronger, more loving and patient people.

Free will

Christians believe that when God created people he gave them **free will**, the ability to be able to make choices for themselves, including the decision to act in a good or evil way. Therefore evil and suffering can be the result of the choices people make.

Suffering happens for a reason

Another response Christians may give to the existence of evil and suffering is to say that it is part of God's plan – he knows why everything happens and we cannot. Suffering may be part of God's ultimate plan and therefore people should trust in God.

Activities

A tsunami victim.

Tsunami victims receiving aid.

1 The photographs show: (i) a tsunami victim, and (ii) charity workers helping the needy afterwards.

'Good always comes out of evil.' Do you agree? Give your reasons.

Many Christians would also say that suffering allows people to follow Jesus's example and do good works. This is illustrated by the two images on this page. The Asian Tsunami in December 2004 brought terrible suffering and destruction. Afterwards, however, the result was a great deal of good works as people sent unprecedented amounts of charity in the form of money or gifts. Some people actually went to the affected areas to help out too.

ResultsPlus
Exam question report

Choose one religion and explain how its followers respond to the problem of evil and suffering. (8 marks) June 2007

How students answered

Many candidates scored poorly on this question because they did not identify with any one religion and their answer was generally about the problem of evil and suffering.

Most of the candidates who scored three or four marks for this question identified a religion and then focused on one response.

There were some excellent answers, which gave a detailed response to some of the different ways in which believers, from the religion the candidate had chosen, deal with the problem of evil and suffering. The best answers offered several different responses and explained them.

Summary

- Christians attempt to solve the problem of evil by explaining why God permits evil and suffering even when he could, if all-powerful, remove it.
- Some argue that it is a test from God to bring people closer to him.
- Others use the Bible (Genesis 1–3) to explain how suffering came into the world through people's exercise of their free will.

1.11 The media and belief in God

Learning outcomes

By the end of this lesson, you should be able to:

● name and describe some media programmes about religion

● evaluate how these programmes could affect attitudes to believing in God.

For this course you need to know two examples of media programmes that might affect a person's attitude to belief in God. These can be TV shows, radio shows or films. On television, programmes about religion take various forms. A few are directed at religious believers offering them worship and teaching, for example *Songs of Praise*. Many more are also of interest to non-believers. These can be comedy shows such as *The Vicar of Dibley* or documentaries such as *Tsunami - Where was God?*.

Other programmes are less obviously connected to religion but could still affect a viewer's attitudes to belief in God. Examples include dramas or soap operas which may feature characters who follow a religious faith or which sometimes have storylines about religion. You do not just have to focus on television shows. Many films such as *Bruce Almighty* or *The Da Vinci Code* may affect a person's attitude to belief in God.

An edition of Songs of Praise.

The influence of the media

The media can have a powerful influence over all of our lives without us even realising it! Most people have the radio or television on at some point every day and the Internet means that they can also access the media when they are away from home.

When it comes to presenting religion, some programmes show religious belief as a positive thing to be encouraged. They may show that belief in God can benefit a person and fulfil their life.

Alternatively, programmes can show religious belief more negatively and present it as something to laugh at and ridicule. They may suggest that people who believe in God are crazy, slightly strange or even dangerous. How much does the media portrayal of religious belief affect our attitudes?

People aren't stupid. They know that TV dramas and soaps are just made up to entertain us. Nobody would expect all Christians to act like Dot Cotton in *Eastenders*.

TV shows might be made up, but soaps and stuff are still based on reality. Some people get so caught up in them that they do believe the characters are real and then they might want to be like them or not.

I think the media affects everyone hugely, even though we don't like to admit it. If we see loads of programmes like The Vicar of Dibley where the Christians are all weird, then that's bound to affect our views of Christians generally.

I don't think anyone would watch a TV show or a film and from that change their minds about religious believers or whether they believe in God or not. People make up their own minds; they don't need TV to help them!

Summary

• The media show many programmes that portray people believing in God as well as showing different attitudes to religions.

• This can have an effect on whether people think they should believe in God or not.

examzone

Know Zone
Believing in God

Quick quiz

1 What is meant by 'omnipotent'?

2 What is meant by 'omniscient'?

3 How might the family help people believe in God?

4 Give two other ways in which people may come to believe in God.

5 Give an example of how a Christian might experience a miracle.

6 What is a conversion experience?

7 What is meant by 'causation'?

8 Why do some people think that unanswered prayer affects belief in God?

9 Define the two types of evil and suffering.

10 Suggest two ways in which Christians might respond to suffering.

Plenary activity

Create two characters, any age, gender, race, background or circumstances. One is an atheist, one a theist (believer in God). Using all the topics in this section, write a short report about each character, filling in their personal details as suggested above, and explaining what they believe.

For example, you could create a character named Alan, who is in his mid-thirties, brought up in a Christian home, but who now describes himself as an atheist. Why has he stopped believing in God? Did he ever believe for himself? What does he think about suffering in the world, prayer, the possible causes for the origin of the world, and so on?

Find out more

For more information on the topics below go to www.heinemann.co.uk/hotlinks (express code 4196P) and click on the appropriate link.

- **Religious facts:** Find out more about different Christian groups or denominations in the world.
- **Popular evangelists**: Find out more about Benny Hinn to decide whether God works miracles today.
- **Creation**: Interesting items and video clips for further reading.
- **Origins**: Interesting NASA website with some fine photographs for further reading.
- **Evolution**: Lots of pictures and information for further reading.
- **BBC programmes about religion**: Find out more about BBC religious programmes.
- **Programmes about religion on Channel 4**: Find out more about Channel 4 television programmes that deal with key issues of religious belief.

Take the opportunity to pick up leaflets in churches and other places of worship or where Christians meet together. These will often deal with questions people have about faith, or they may advertise events that could give you a greater insight into why people believe and what they do together. For example, many Churches run religious courses, which teach the fundamentals of the Christian faith.

Student tips

When I studied these topics for my GCSE, I made sure that I knew all the specification key words very well. This was so I could be sure of getting full marks for all the questions that asked for meanings of key words, but also so I could use some of them in other answers to show my understanding of the topics. For example, I could use 'omnipotent' when writing about why religious believers have to find solutions to the problem of evil, even if there wasn't a short question asking what that word means.

Self-evaluation checklist

Read through the following list and evaluate how well you know and understand each of the topics.
How well have you understood the topics in this section? In the first column of the table below use the
following code to rate your understanding:

Green – I understand this fully

Orange – I am confident I can answer most questions on this

Red – I need to do a lot more work on this topic.

In the second and third columns you need to think about:

● Whether you have an opinion on this topic and could give reasons for that opinion if asked

● Whether you can give the opinion of someone who disagrees with you and give reasons for this
alternative opinion.

Content covered	My understanding is red/orange/ green	Can I give my opinion?	Can I give an alternative opinion?
● The importance of a religious upbringing in coming to believe in God			
● The ways in which a religious family can encourage children to believe in God			
● How religious communities contribute to a religious upbringing			
● The nature of religious experiences			
● Different types of religious experiences			
● What people believe about religious experiences			
● What is understood by the term 'miracle'			
● Different types of miracles			
● Why God may perform miracles			
● Problems associated with miracles			
● The nature of prayer			
● Why believers associate prayer with the nature of God			
● The design argument for the existence of God			
● The argument for the existence of God based on causation			
● What it means to be a theist, atheist or agnostic			
● Why some people feel that science offers a better explanation of the origin of the world, with the result that they do not believe in God			
● Some scientific explanations of the origin of the world			
● Ways in which Christians respond to scientific explanations for the origin of the world			
● The nature of evil and suffering and why they may cause problems for religious believers			
● Ways in which Christians attempt to solve the problems of evil and suffering			
● Some programmes about religion shown on television			
● How those programmes may aim to influence people's views about religion			
● The range of radio programmes about religion, their aims and content			

exam zone

Know Zone
Believing in God

Introduction

In the exam you will see a choice of two questions on this section. Each question will include four tasks, which test your knowledge, understanding and evaluation of the material covered. A 2-mark question will ask you to define a term; a 4-mark question will ask your opinion on a point of view; an 8-mark question will ask you to explain a particular belief or idea; a 6-mark question will ask for your opinion on a point of view and ask you to consider an alternative point of view.

Mini exam paper

(a) What is **atheism?** (2 marks)

(b) Do you think prayer is a waste of time?
Give **two** reasons for your point of view. (4 marks)

(c) Explain how a religious upbringing can lead to belief in God. (8 marks)

(d) *'Evil and suffering prove that God does not exist.'*
In your answer you should refer to at least one religion.
(i) Do you agree? Give reasons for your opinion. (3 marks)
(ii) Give reasons why some people may disagree with you. (3 marks)

You must give your opinion, but make sure you do give two clear and properly thought-out reasons. These can be ones you have learned in class, even if they are not your own opinion. You mustn't use terms such as 'rubbish' or 'stupid' as these don't show that you are able to think things through carefully.

In your answer you should state whether or not you agree with the statement. You should also give reasons for your opinion.

Here you need to give a short, accurate definition. You do not need to write more than one clear sentence.

The word 'explain' means you should give details of activities religious families may carry out together or ways in which they share their faith, but you must also show how these may lead to belief in God. This question is worth 8 marks so you must be prepared to spend some time answering it. You will also be assessed on your use of language in this question.

Now you have to give the opposite point of view, again using material you have learned during your studies. You don't have to say what you think about these alternative points of view, but you do need to show you understand why they are just as important to consider as your own opinion.

Mark scheme

(a) You can earn **2 marks** for a correct answer, and **1 mark** for a partially correct answer.

(b) To earn up to the full **4 marks** you need to give two reasons and develop them fully. Two brief reasons or only one without any development will earn **2 marks**.

(c) You can earn **7–8 marks** by giving up to four reasons, but the fewer reasons you give, the more you must develop them. Because you are being assessed on use of language, you also need to take care to express your understanding in a clear style of English, and make some use of specialist vocabulary.

(d) To go beyond **3 marks** for the whole of this question you must refer to at least one religion. The more you are able to develop your reasons the more marks you will earn. Three simple reasons can earn you the same mark as one fully developed reason.

ResultsPlus
Maximise your marks

(b)   Do you think prayer is a waste of time? Give **two** reasons for your point of view. (4 marks)

Student answer	Examiner comments	Improved student answer
I think that prayer is not a waste of time as it is a way to make contact with God. Even though God cannot be seen or heard in the usual way, believers in God can speak to him through prayer and believe that he is listening.	The phrase 'a way to make contact with God' is good, and the answer comments on the difficulty of knowing God, with prayer offering one way of solving that difficulty.	I think prayer is not a waste of time as it is a way to make contact with God. A person may pray for their friends or relatives, and will feel better in the knowledge that they have done something to try to help them.
There is always the chance that he may answer the believer's prayer and make their lives better.	The candidate comes close to giving another reason by saying that prayer may make the believer's life better, but it hasn't really been explained. This answer will gain 3 marks as the candidate has given only one reason that has been developed.	The more a person prays, their belief in God will become stronger, as they understand that God hears them and cares about them.

Matters of life and death

Introduction

In this section you will learn about major issues that concern many people, not just religious believers – issues of life and death. We will all die at some point, but for religious believers what happens after death is crucially important, as are the ways that we deal with life on Earth. How highly do we value life and what steps do we take to improve it and protect it? In this section you will learn how Christians and Muslims go about answering these questions.

Learning outcomes for this section

By the end of this section you should be able to:

- Give definitions of the key words and use them in answers to GCSE questions
- Explain why Christians and Muslims believe in life after death and how these beliefs affect the way they live their lives
- Outline non-religious reasons for believing in life after death (near-death experiences, ghosts, mediums, evidence of reincarnation)
- Explain why some people do not believe in life after death
- Outline the current law on abortion in the United Kingdom, and explain why abortion is a controversial issue
- Describe Christian and Muslim attitudes to abortion, explaining why there are differences
- Outline the current law on euthanasia in the United Kingdom, and explain why euthanasia is a controversial issue
- Describe Christian and Muslim attitudes to euthanasia, explaining why there are differences
- Explain how an issue raised in this section (abortion, euthanasia or life after death) has been presented in the media
- Describe arguments for and against the media being free to criticise what religions say about matters of life and death
- Express with reasons and evidence your own opinion about the issues covered in this section.

edexcel ▦ key terms

abortion	**paranormal**
assisted suicide	**quality of life**
euthanasia	**reincarnation**
immortality of the soul	**resurrection**
near-death experience	**sanctity of life**
non-voluntary euthanasia	**voluntary euthanasia**

The picture shows part of the Last Judgement by Michelangelo. The whole painting covers a wall in the Sistine Chapel in the Vatican. The top of the painting is Heaven and the bottom is Hell – which part do you think is shown here?

In the class as a whole, or in small groups or pairs, find out what people feel about issues of abortion and euthanasia. Take a poll or ask for motions, such as 'We believe abortion should be available on demand' or 'Life is precious and should not be taken under any circumstances'. Find out how many of the class agree or disagree with these claims and why.

After you have studied this section return to your responses and see if anyone's opinions have changed.

Fascinating fact

According to a survey done by *Dignity with Dying*, 80 per cent of the public think it is unacceptable that people who are suffering unbearably from a terminal illness cannot ask for medical help to die if that is what they want.

2.1 Christian beliefs in life after death and how it affects the way Christians live

Learning outcomes

By the end of this lesson, you should be able to:

- describe the different beliefs about life after death held by Christians
- explain why Christians have different beliefs about life after death
- explain why Christians believe in life after death
- understand how these beliefs affect the way they live their lives.

edexcel ⦂⦂⦂ key terms

Immortality of the soul – The idea that the soul lives on after the death of the body.

Resurrection – The belief that, after death, the body stays in the grave until the end of the world when it is raised.

Glossary

Heaven – A place of paradise where God rules.

Hell – A place of horrors where Satan rules.

Purgatory – Roman Catholic belief in a place where those who do not go straight to Heaven go into a state of waiting and preparation for Heaven where their souls will be cleansed.

Activities

1 Consider what each of these images says about life after death. Which one is the closest representation to your own belief about life after death? Give your reasons.

2 Create your own picture expressing your feelings about death and the afterlife. It could be a symbolic collection of colours and words or just a simple drawing. Write a short explanation of how you came to your final design.

3 For those who believe in life after death, what is it that lives on?

Christian beliefs

All Christians believe in life after death. They all agree that Jesus died and rose from the dead and that there will be an afterlife for those who love and believe in him. Their evidence for life after death comes from the **resurrection** of Jesus, the teachings of the Bible and of the Church (the Creed). However, Christians have different views about what happens when you die. Most believe in either the **immortality of the soul** or the resurrection of the body.

Christian beliefs in life after death

Who	They believe what	Why
Many Protestant Christians	They believe that after death the body will stay in the grave, but the soul will go straight to God for judgement. There is a difference of opinion about what will happen to those who do not go to Heaven, and some believe there is no such place as Hell.	• Jesus told a thief on the cross that he would be in Heaven that day (Luke 23:43). • Jesus said his father's house had many rooms that Jesus was preparing for his followers (John 14:2). • The teaching of the Church is that there can be a communion of the saints (communication between dead and living Christians). • There is, for example, evidence of the paranormal, such as ghosts and mediums.
Other Evangelical Protestant Christians	They believe that after death the body and soul stay in the grave until the end of the world. At this time a Christian will be judged. The good will go to Heaven and sinners who have not repented will go to Hell.	• Jesus's body was raised from the dead (Luke 24:39). • The Creed says *'I believe in the resurrection of the body and the everlasting life.'* • St Paul teaches this belief in 1 Corinthians 15:42–44.
Roman Catholic Christians	They believe in both the resurrection of the body and immortality of the soul. They believe that the soul of a Christian who has not sinned since their last confession will go straight to Heaven. The soul of a Christian who has sinned will go to purgatory for their souls to be cleansed. The souls who do not believe in God or have committed unforgivable sins will go to Hell. After this, Jesus will come back to Earth to raise the dead and reunite their bodies and souls. God will make a new Heaven and a new Earth and the souls in purgatory will go to Heaven and the souls from Hell will return to Hell.	• The resurrection of Jesus. • The teachings of the New Testament. • The teaching in the Catechism of the Catholic Church. • The Creed, which says Jesus *'is seated at the right hand of the father and will come again to judge the living and the dead'*.

Activities

4 If you were to add your opinion at the end of this chart, what would it be?

• The promise of Heaven offers an explanation for suffering experienced in this life.
• The promise of the afterlife means forgiveness for Christians who have repented, and new hope for a better future.

The effect on Christians' lives

Belief in life after death affects the way Christians live their lives.

• Christians believe that they will be judged by God after death, so they live within the guidelines given in the Bible and by the Church. This affects how they live and how they treat others.
• The fact that Jesus rose from the dead gives them hope that they will also rise, and that they will be rewarded for their time on Earth.
• It offers comfort to those who have suffered the death of a loved one.

Summary

• All Christians believe in life after death.
• There are a variety of Christian views about what happens. Most Christians believe in either the immortality of the soul or the resurrection of the body.
• This affects how Christians live their lives because they believe God will reward those who have lived according to God's will.

2.2 Islamic beliefs about life after death

Learning outcomes

By the end of this lesson, you should be able to:

- describe what Muslims believe about the afterlife
- explain how Muslim beliefs about the afterlife affect their lives on Earth
- give your own opinions on these issues.

Glossary

Akhirah – Life after death.

al'Jannah – Heaven.

Hadith – The sayings of the Prophet.

Jahannam – Hell.

Qur'an – Sacred book of Islam.

Akhirah

Belief in *akhirah*, or life after death, is very important for Muslims. They believe that the angel of death will first take a person's soul to *barzakh*, which is the stage between the moment they die and the moment of facing judgement.

Like many Christians, Muslims believe that the body will be resurrected on the Day of Judgement.

As a result of judgement, they will be sent to Paradise (*al'Jannah*) or to Hell (*jahannam*). This decision is made when two angels open the book which contains the record of what a person has done in their lifetime. If their name is recorded on the right-hand side of the book, they will be sent to Paradise, but if it is recorded on the left-hand side, they will be sent to Hell. Unfortunately, while all people will try to reach Paradise over the Assirat Bridge, those whose destiny is to go to Hell will fall off in the attempt.

Whether a person will remain for eternity in either Heaven or Hell is entirely up to Allah: '*Their status in Heaven and Hell may last for eternity, but this is subject to God's will and mercy*' (Surah 11:106–108).

What is the afterlife like?

Muhammad's Paradise, *miniature from* The History of Muhammad.

Activities

1 Why are beliefs in the afterlife so important to Muslims?

2 What does this painting of Paradise tell us about what will happen according to Islam?

For discussion

If God is merciful, then why does he send people to Hell?

The Qur'an makes use of strong descriptions of *al'Jannah* (Heaven) and *jahannam* (Hell). Heaven is described as a beautiful garden, full of wonderful leaves and flowers, where soothing sounds of birds singing and water running can be heard, while the blessed will enjoy the company of beautiful women as they eat delicious food. Those who are destined for *jahannam*, however, will face terrible torments of fire and smoke as they face eternal punishments, chained up and burned by boiling water and painful biting winds.

Surah 56:115–121 teaches that those who live a good life will

'… *sit on gold-encrusted thrones of happiness… Immortal youths will wait upon them with… cups filled with water from pure springs… and with fruit of any kind that they choose…*'

Although these descriptions are very graphic, not all Muslims believe that they are literally true, but rather they understand them as metaphors. It is impossible to know what Heaven and Hell are really like, or even if they exist in a literal way, but the images which are used are a good way of making them seem real.

Activities

3 Write a paragraph summarising Muslim beliefs about life after death. How similar or different are they from your own views?

Judgement

Obviously, no Muslim wants to go to Hell, and the key to ensuring that they will enjoy the blessings of Heaven is to follow the teachings of the Qur'an and the Shari'ah law. The Shari'ah law is based partially on the Qur'an, but also on the teachings of the Prophet Muhammad and the work of Islamic scholars (Hadith). Muslims believe their Earthly life is observed by Allah, and that everything they do and say is recorded and assessed for the afterlife. Islamic belief in the resurrection means that Muslims are not cremated, but are buried so that their body is ready to be raised by God.

For discussion

Is Heaven only for religious people?

Although some Muslims believe that *only* Muslims will go to Heaven (in the same way that some Christians believe only Christians can be saved), others allow that non-Muslims (particularly believers of the other Abrahamic faiths, which are Judaism and Christianity) who have led morally good lives may also go to Heaven.

In the afterlife, the good will be rewarded and the evil punished, and the moral law will be balanced so that those who suffered unfairly in this life will receive compensation for injustice. There must be consequences, good or bad, for everything done on Earth:

'*The unbelievers say, "Never to us will come the hour"… But most surely, he may reward those who believe and work deeds of righteousness, for such is forgiveness and a sustenance most generous. But those who strive against our signs, to frustrate them, for such will be a chastisement, of painful wrath.*' (Surah 34:3–5)

God's judgement is final:

'*Until, when death comes to one of them, he says "O, my Lord! Send me back to life, in order that I may work righteousness in the things I neglected". By no means… The fire will burn their faces and they will therein grin with their lips displaced.*' (Surah 23:99–104)

Summary

- The idea of *akhirah* is a central belief in Islam.
- Muslims believe that those who follow the teachings of the Qur'an, the sayings of the Prophet and the Hadith will go to Heaven, having passed through God's judgement. In Heaven they will enjoy many blessings.
- In Hell, those who have not followed God's ways will suffer eternal torments.

2.3 Non-religious belief in life after death

Learning outcomes

By the end of this lesson, you should be able to:

- understand and explain why non-religious believers think there may be an afterlife
- describe the different possible types of afterlife
- describe a near-death experience
- give your opinion and the reasons for it.

edexcel ⠿ key terms

Near-death experience – When someone about to die has an out-of-body experience.

Paranormal – Unexplained things that are thought to have spiritual causes

Reincarnation – The belief that, after death, souls are reborn in a new body.

Why do people believe in an afterlife?

Many people who are not religious still hope that there will be another life after they die. Some reasons for this are given in these speech bubbles:

> We find the idea of death very difficult to cope with.

> We need to feel that something of who we are carries on after physical death.

> Sometimes we feel our deceased loved ones are still with us.

> Earthly life is so unfair – an afterlife will make everything right.

> Those who lead a good life should be rewarded and those who are bad should be punished.

> Some people have claimed to experience life after death through a near-death experience.

A nineteenth-century image of a ghost, a time when these sorts of images were very popular.

Activities

1. Make a list of as many reasons as you can think of for saying that there *is* life after death. Now make a list of as many reasons as you can think of for saying that there *is no* afterlife.

2. Which list, in your view, contains the most convincing arguments, and why?

Activities

3. Many people claim to have seen a ghost. Do you think that ghosts are real? Give your reasons.

Experiences of an afterlife

Near-death experiences
These have been reported by patients who have been pronounced dead for a small amount of time. They describe leaving their bodies and seeing themselves from outside of their body. In some cases they report seeing relatives and friends who have already died or a bright light they feel they want to travel towards.
They are convinced this is evidence that there is an afterlife.

Ghosts
These are thought to be the spirits of dead people who for some reason have not travelled on to the 'next place'. They can either be a physical presence which can be seen or a sense or feeling of someone being in room with you. It is believed some ghosts haunt the living, others come to support and look after loved ones, and others try to contact the living.

Some people claim to have experienced paranormal activities.

Contacting the dead
People such as mediums claim to be able to contact the dead. Contacting the dead was banned in the Bible and had a very severe punishment: '*A man or woman who is a medium or spiritualist among you must be put to death*' (Leviticus 20:27). Many people attend meetings (called seances) at which they attempt to contact the dead and believe that they have actually done this. Others claim these meetings are situations made up by people who wish to take advantage of the grief of others. On some Sky channels you can watch mediums pass messages on from the dead.

Reincarnation
This is the belief that a person's soul is reborn into another body or form when they die. This is often seen as a religious thing because it is believed by Hindus and Sikhs but many non-religious people also believe in reincarnation because of déjà vu or memories from past lives.

For discussion
What do you think about the evidence of life after death from a non-religious point of view? Do you believe in ghosts, the power of mediums or stories of near-death experiences? What are your reasons for this point of view?

Summary
- Many non-religious people believe in an afterlife in which the human spirit lives on after the death of the body.
- This belief may be supported by things such as ghosts, mediums and near-death experiences.

2.4 Non-belief in life after death

Learning outcomes

By the end of this lesson, you should be able to:

● understand and explain why some people reject belief in an afterlife

● explain why they may do so for different reasons

● express your own opinion and give reasons for it.

Many non-religious people do not believe in any form of the afterlife. This can be for several different reasons:

● They believe there is no evidence for an afterlife
● They believe that religion offers no good reasons to believe in an afterlife
● They believe that mediums and other people who attempt to prove there is an afterlife are tricking people
● They believe that in an age when science explains the world, we should not believe in things that are unscientific
● When a person dies their body decays, so how can they live again?
● Life after death is simply impossible – we are either alive or dead.

Activities

1 Explain the reasons why non-religious people may not believe in an afterlife. In your opinion, which of the reasons are convincing, and why?

These ideas are not simply about the problems of belief in the afterlife, but are also about what we think about being human beings. If we think that to be human is to be physical and mortal, we will find it impossible to believe in an afterlife, in which we are spiritual and immortal.

Although, as we have seen, it is possible to believe in an afterlife without being religious, some non-believers think that it is impossible to believe in an afterlife without believing in God.

Mediums and spiritualists who conduct seances (or sessions with individuals in which they apparently communicate with the spirits of the dead) can be seen as simply playing on the sad circumstances of those who are bereaved. Many have been exposed as frauds, adding to the claims of non-believers that there is no real evidence of the afterlife.

For discussion

What do you think? Can you believe in an afterlife without believing in God?

Activities

2 Why, in your opinion, are so many people convinced by mediums?

3 Do you think that it is possible to contact the dead? Give your reasons.

4 'Death is the end. There is nothing else.' Do you agree? Give reasons for your viewpoint.

Beliefs in Heaven and Hell are central to many religions, however for many non-believers these are outdated ideas. Some people argue that religions use the idea of Heaven and Hell to control people's behaviour. Many years ago, it was usual for Christian Churches to teach believers about Hell in order to frighten them and hence control their behaviour. If people didn't want to go to Hell, then they had to believe what the Church told them, and, sometimes, Churches were teaching ideas that benefited the Churches more than their members.

For discussion

● In your opinion, do ghosts exist?
● Would the existence of ghosts prove that there is life after death?

This is supposedly the image of a ghost at Hampton Court. What do you think?

ResultsPlus
Exam question report

Explain why some people do not believe in life after death (8 marks) (June 2007)

How students answered

Many students scored poorly on this question because they answered very vaguely. Some wrote about why people do not believe in life after death, which would have received no marks.

These answers generally offered one developed reason or a couple of brief reasons but not enough to gain high marks

There were some students who gave excellent answers to this question. They either gave three or four reasons, or developed at least two reasons.

Summary

- Many non-believers reject belief in an afterlife because there is no evidence for it and because in today's modern world beliefs in the afterlife do not make sense.
- Others reject it because it is used as a means of controlling the behaviour and choices of believers.
- Some reject ideas of Heaven and Hell.
- Others reject the afterlife because it is inconsistent with what it means to be human.

2.5 Abortion

Learning outcomes

By the end of this lesson, you should be able to:

● understand what is meant by abortion and why it is controversial

● explain different views on when life begins

● understand the current UK legislation on abortion

● give your own opinions on abortion law and the reasons for them.

edexcel ::: **key terms**

Abortion – The removal of a foetus from the womb before it can survive.

What is abortion?

An **abortion** takes place when the life of the foetus is ended in the womb. We use the word to refer to the ending of a pregnancy by surgical or medical means. When a pregnancy ends naturally before the foetus is ready to be born, it is called a miscarriage.

Debates about abortion are very controversial because there are many different opinions about when life actually begins and whether it is ever right to kill.

So, when does life begin? Different people believe that life begins at the following times:

● At fertilisation
● When the fertilised egg is implanted into the wall of the womb
● When the foetus is in the womb
● When the foetus is capable of living independently of the mother
● At birth.

A 16-week-old foetus in the womb. In your opinion, is it a human being? Give your reasons.

The UK abortion laws

The current law on abortion is based on the 1967 Abortion Act and the Human Fertilisation and Embryology Act of 1990. Before 1967 abortion was illegal in the UK.

Under the present law abortion is allowed *up to 24 weeks* (of the pregnancy) if:

● continuing with the pregnancy would pose a risk to the physical or mental health of the woman
● the physical or mental health of the woman's existing children would suffer if a new baby were born
● if the child were born it would be seriously mentally or physically handicapped.

Abortion is allowed *after 24 weeks* (of the pregnancy) if there is:

● risk to the life of the woman
● evidence that the baby will be severely deformed
● risk of serious physical and mental injury to the woman.

All abortions must be agreed by two doctors (one in an emergency) and carried out by a doctor in a government-approved NHS or private hospital or clinic.

There were 198,500 abortions in 2007 compared with 193,700 in 2006. The largest number of abortions were carried out on 19-year-old women, while 4.4 per cent of abortions were carried out on girls under 16 and 19.8

per cent on girls under 18 years old. There have been 6.7 million legal abortions in the UK since 1967.

Go to www.heinemann.co.uk/hotlinks (express code 4196P) for more information on the UK abortion laws.

Arguments for and against abortion

People who believe that the mother should be able to choose whether to have an abortion are called 'pro-choice'. People who believe that the child has a right to life are called 'pro-life'. Let's look at what these people believe in more detail.

ResultsPlus
Exam question report

Explain why people argue about abortion. (8 marks) June 2007

How students answered

Most of the candidates who scored poorly on this question tried to answer the question from the point of view of one religion – which is *not* what the question required.

Many candidates could explain a few of the reasons why abortion is controversial, but did not go into enough detail or explain the opposing view. Some did not include the points of view of religious believers.

Many candidates scored well on this question because they explained the controversy about abortion. They gave specific examples (e.g. when does life begin?) and explained how different people, including religious believers, respond to these issues.

Summary

- Abortion is the termination of the life of the foetus in the womb.
- Although abortion is legal in the UK, it is controversial because people have different views on when life begins.
- Abortion is allowed up to 24 weeks (of the pregancy) in certain conditions, and after 24 weeks if the risk to life and health is severe.

Activities

1 Read Preeti's arguments for abortion and Callum's arguments against.

2 What do you think about Callum's arguments for pro-life?

3 What do you think about Preeti's arguments for pro-choice?

4 Draw yourself in the middle of a page and put your own speech bubbles around showing what you think about abortion and explaining why.

2.6 Christian attitudes to abortion

Learning outcomes

By the end of this lesson, you should be able to:

● understand different Christian attitudes to abortion

● explain why Christians have these different views

● give your own opinions on these different views and the reasons for them.

edexcel ⋮⋮⋮ key terms

Sanctity of life – The belief that life is holy and belongs to God.

Sanctity of life

Christians do not all share the same views about abortion. However, most Christians will not support abortion because of the principle of the **sanctity of life.** This means that life is sacred, or holy, and that it is a gift from God. Christians believe that God has a very special relationship with human beings because they are made in his image and have responsibility over the rest of creation.

There are important passages in the Bible which support this view:

> 'So God created man in his own image. In the image of God he created him: male and female, he created them.' (Genesis 1:27)

> 'Your body is a temple of the Holy Spirit, who is in you, whom you have received from God. You are not on your own... therefore honour God with your body.' (1 Corinthians 6:19–20)

> 'You shall not commit murder.' (Exodus 20:13)

Activities

1 What does the 'sanctity of life' mean?

2 How does believing in the sanctity of life affect a person's view on abortion?

Christians protesting against abortion.

Conservative Christian views

Conservative Christians (typically most Roman Catholics and evangelical Protestant groups) are against abortion on the grounds that every human being has the right to life.

The teaching of the Roman Catholic Church is very clear on abortion:

'God alone is the Lord of life… no one can under any circumstances claim for himself the right directly to destroy an innocent human being.' (Catechism of the Catholic Church)

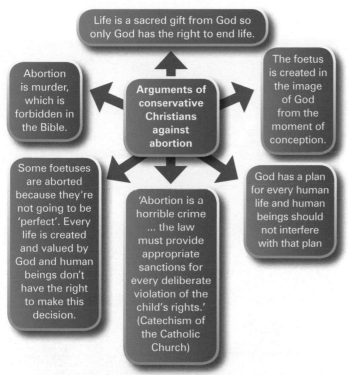

Life is a sacred gift from God so only God has the right to end life.

Abortion is murder, which is forbidden in the Bible.

The foetus is created in the image of God from the moment of conception.

Arguments of conservative Christians against abortion

Some foetuses are aborted because they're not going to be 'perfect'. Every life is created and valued by God and human beings don't have the right to make this decision.

'Abortion is a horrible crime … the law must provide appropriate sanctions for every deliberate violation of the child's rights.' (Catechism of the Catholic Church)

God has a plan for every human life and human beings should not interfere with that plan

For discussion

Are there any situations in which a conservative Christian would be forced to accept that an abortion might be the right thing to do?

Other Christian views

The Church of England is more liberal about this issue, agreeing abortion is not a good thing, but allowing that it may sometimes be a better choice or even the most loving thing to do. For example, in cases of rape or incest, or when the mother's life is seriously at risk.

The General Synod, the governing body of the Church of England, states:

'The Church of England combines strong opposition to abortion with a recognition that there can be – strictly limited – conditions under which it may be morally preferable to any available alternative.'

The Church of England also believes that when an abortion is the lesser of two evils, it must be carried out as early as possible and the only reason to have an abortion beyond 24 weeks is *'where there is a serious foetal disability and survival will be for a very short period of time'*.

This more liberal view on abortion may be influenced by following ideas:

- Jesus acted with love and compassion and taught his followers to do so. Having one strict rule on abortion, which forbids it in all cases, may be unloving to both mother and child.
- There are cases when the principle of the sanctity of life is broken – for example, in times of war – so abortion may occasionally offer another case when it might also be broken.
- We cannot be sure that life begins at conception.
- Medical technology has advanced so that handicapped foetuses can be identified early enough to avoid later, less traumatic abortions.

Activities

3 What does the 'lesser of two evils' mean?

4 Draw a grid summarising the different Christian views on abortion. What do you think of them – which view do you most agree with?

Go to www.heinemann.co.uk/hotlinks (express code 4196P) for more information on Christian attitudes to abortion.

Summary

- Conservative Christians adopt a strict view on abortion, using the principle of the sanctity of life to argue against abortion for any reason.
- More liberal Christians still believe that abortion is not a good thing, but that it may be allowed in situations where it is the lesser of two evils, or the better (although bad) moral choice.

2.7 Muslim attitudes to abortion

Learning outcomes

By the end of this lesson, you should be able to:

● understand different Muslim attitudes to abortion

● explain why Muslims have these different views

● give your own opinions on these different views and the reasons for them.

Activities

1 Given what you have learned about Muslim beliefs about life after death, explain why ensoulment is so important to Muslims in relation to their views on abortion.

2 'The life of the mother is more important than the life of the foetus'. Why might a Muslim allow abortion if the mother's life is in danger?

The sanctity of life and ensoulment

Muslims share similar views to Christians on the principle of the sanctity of life. Life to Muslims is sacred and a gift from God. Abortion is considered to be wrong because it is taking away a life.

'Whosoever has spared the life of a soul, it is as though he has spared the life of all people. Whosoever has killed a soul, it is as though he has murdered all of mankind.' (Qur'an 5:32)

Many Muslims believe that a life begins once the soul has entered the foetus. This is known as ensoulment and takes place when the foetus is 120 days (or 16 weeks) old. However, there is some disagreement among Muslim scholars as to when life begins. Although most claim 120 days, some claim as early as 40 days, and some when there is movement of the foetus.

Muslim views on abortion

Muslims believe that abortion is wrong but many agree that it might be allowed in some cases.

All Muslims accept that it can be permitted if the mother's life is in danger, and this is the only reason that it can take place after 120 days. This is seen as the lesser of two evils because:

● The foetus wouldn't exist if it weren't for the mother and if she dies, in most cases the foetus will die anyway.

● The mother's life is already established and she has responsibilities to carry out.

● She is part of a family.

For discussion

Children experiencing extreme poverty.

Should abortion be allowed in circumstances of extreme poverty, such as this picture shows? Give reasons for your answer.

Different schools of Muslim thought have varying views on whether there are any other permitted reasons for abortion and when they may take place.

- Some schools of Muslim law allow abortion in the first 16 weeks of pregnancy, others only in the first seven weeks.
- The widest held view is that before 120 days a foetus suffering from a serious, untreatable defect or a genetic blood disorder can be aborted. Some allow this to be extended to include a deformity if two doctors agree that the deformity would mean the child could not live a normal life.
- Some Muslim scholars say abortion is permitted when the mother has been raped or the foetus is due to incest, but others still claim it is not permitted despite those circumstances.
- Abortion is never permitted when the parents are afraid that they cannot care for it.
  '*Kill not your offspring for fear of poverty; it is we who provide for them and for you. Surely, killing them is a great sin.*' (Qur'an 17:32).
- The pregnancy wasn't planned or because it will be inconvenient to the mother.
- The woman becomes pregnant after committing adultery.

Activities

3   Make a list of all the arguments concerning abortion from the Christian point of view. Then make a list of the Muslim points of view.

4   In what ways are the Christian and Muslim views the same? In what ways are they different?

For discussion

- Explain the reasons for differing points of view in Islam.
- Should a Muslim woman be free to have an abortion if she chooses?

Summary

- Most Muslims believe that abortion is always wrong, but most agree that it can be permitted before 120 days if the woman's life is in danger or the foetus will be seriously disabled.
- After 120 days, the only permitted reason is to save the mother's life.
- Although abortion is considered wrong in Islam, it is a compassionate religion and therefore allows some flexibility.

2.8 Euthanasia

Learning outcomes

By the end of this lesson, you should be able to:

- understand what is meant by euthanasia and be able to describe different types
- explain why some people believe that euthanasia should be legalised
- explain why some people are for euthanasia in some situations
- offer your own opinion and understand why some people will have different opinions.

edexcel ⠿ key terms

Assisted suicide – Providing a seriously ill person with the means to commit suicide.

Euthanasia – The painless killing of someone dying from a painful disease.

Non-voluntary euthanasia – Ending someone's life painlessly when they are unable to ask, but you have good reason for thinking they would want you to do so.

Voluntary euthanasia – Ending life painlessly when someone in great pain asks for death.

Euthanasia is a Greek word which literally means 'good death' and is also more generally known as 'easy death' or 'mercy killing'. It is a very important issue in medical ethics today and although many people are against it, there is growing support for euthanasia. In some countries, such as the Netherlands, it is not against the law.

There are several types of euthanasia and several ways in which it may be carried out.

- **Voluntary euthanasia** is when a person's life is deliberately ended at their request. Examples could be giving someone an injection which ends their life.
- **Assisted suicide** is the process of providing someone else with the means to end their life. An example could be buying the drugs for someone to take.
- **Non-voluntary euthanasia** is when a person is unable to ask for death, for example because they are 'brain-dead', but they are helped to die because it is believed that this is what they would have wanted.

- Active euthanasia is carried out by a doctor performing a deliberate action, such as a legal injection.
- Passive euthanasia is carried out when medical treatment or life support is deliberately withdrawn or when a severely ill person is not given treatment which would help them to survive.

For discussion

- Is it right to ask a doctor to kill you? Think of the reasons for and against.
- 'Doctors are there to cure, not kill.' Do you agree? Give your reasons.

In the United Kingdom, all forms of euthanasia are against the law. However, switching off a life-support machine for a patient who has already been tested and shown to be 'brain dead' is not euthanasia and is permissible in the United Kingdom.

Arguments for euthanasia

Many people are in favour of euthanasia. They may offer several arguments in support of it:

- It allows the patient to die a gentle, pain-free death and to exercise their right to die as they choose.
- The patient dies with dignity, rather than slowly getting worse, mentally and physically.
- Euthanasia saves medical costs.

- Medical staff can focus their attention on patients who have a chance of recovery.
- It relieves the family of emotional and financial burdens.

Arguments against euthanasia

There are many arguments against euthanasia:

- Whether people are religious or not, many agree with the principle of the sanctity of life and think that it is never acceptable to end someone's life.
- Many see the major problem as the 'slippery slope' argument. This means that if voluntary euthanasia were legalised for the terminally ill who are in severe pain, it would start to be used in other circumstances as well. If this happened, there would be less medical research, which in turn would diminish the value of life even more and put pressure on the sick and dying to choose euthanasia rather than seek a cure.
- Some people might be pressured into choosing euthanasia by their family. In 1993, the House of Lords rejected a proposal to legalise euthanasia, saying: 'It would be next to impossible to ensure that all acts of euthanasia were truly voluntary.'
- Other people, including many doctors, argue that euthanasia is not necessary as death need not be painful and undignified and the work of the hospice movement is dedicated to caring for the terminally sick by concentrating on pain relief to the moment of death.
- Doctors can be wrong about a diagnosis or cures may be found in the future.
- Assisting someone to commit suicide would put a person under a lot of unfair pressure – they would have to live with what they had done for the rest of their life.

Some people feel that one of the disadvantages of medical technology being able to keep people alive for much longer, is that people may be forced to live a poor-quality life where they have to take heavy doses of painkillers from which they may eventually die anyway. This is called the 'principle of double effect' whereby the primary purpose of the painkillers is to relieve pain, but the secondary effect achieved, although not deliberately, is that the patient dies of an overdose.

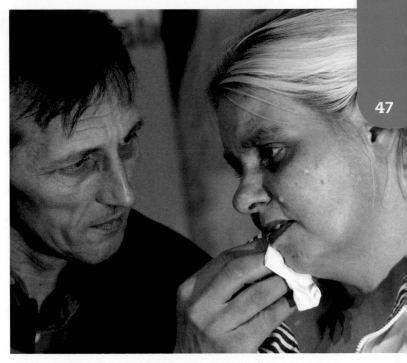

Dianne Pretty was terminally ill and wanted her husband to help her to die. He agreed, but the European Court of Human Rights said that he was not allowed to help her. Dianne Pretty died in 2002, without euthanasia.

Activities

1   Imagine you are in the European Court.
   (a) What arguments would Dianne Pretty have put forward and how would the judge have responded?
   (b) Was the verdict the right one, in your opinion? Give your reasons.

Summary

- Euthanasia, providing a patient with an 'easy death' to avoid long-term pain, is illegal in the UK.
- There are several types of euthanasia. Many people campaign for voluntary euthanasia to be legalised.
- Strong arguments against euthanasia include the view that it undermines the sanctity of life.
- Those in favour argue that the right to die as they wish should be available to all terminally and chronically ill patients.

2.9 Christian attitudes to euthanasia

Learning outcomes

By the end of this lesson, you should be able to:

- understand different Christian attitudes to euthanasia
- explain why Christians have these different views
- give your own opinions on these different views and the reasons for them.

edexcel ::: key terms

Quality of life – The idea that life must have some benefits for it to be worth living.

Euthanasia and the sanctity of life

Like abortion, many Christians object to euthanasia because it goes against the principle of the sanctity of life. For conservative Christians, including Roman Catholics and most evangelicals, it is wrong for the following reasons.

- It is taking away the life of a human being, which is always murder.
- God created human beings in his image, so only he has the power to take away their life.
- Even if a sick person says they want to die, no one has the authority to take their life away.
- Life is so important, it should be valued even when someone is in great pain.
- Terminally ill patients can still worship God and show other people God's love.
- Euthanasia could be used for evil purposes.
- Doctors or relatives may make the choice without consulting the patient.
- No one should be able to make a judgement about the value of another person's life.
- No person should value themselves as so worthless that it would be better to die.

The Roman Catholic Church argues that:

'An act or omission which causes death in order to eliminate suffering constitutes a murder greatly contrary to the dignity of the human person and to the respect due to the living God, his Creator.' (Catechism of the Catholic Church)

Activities

1 Outline different Christian attitudes towards euthanasia.

2 'Euthanasia can never be right.' Do you agree? Give your reasons.

A terminally ill patient

For discussion

- What does it mean to have a 'good quality of life'?
- Why is the sanctity of life so important for Christians?

Can euthanasia ever be the right thing?

However, some Christians are not so strongly opposed to it.

Christians who are more accepting of the possibility of euthanasia may use the argument that God intends that people should have a good **quality of life**. This means that they should be able to do the things that are meaningful to them and make them feel good about life. However, for most Christians, the principle of the sanctity of life outweighs this, and they believe that everyone, however ill or disabled, has a precious life to live.

This is based on the belief that all people are equal, whatever their physical or mental condition, whether they are old, or not even conscious. All people should therefore be treated with dignity.

Activities

4 Explain why a Christian might give money to, or raise money for, their local hospice.

Results Plus

Watch out!

Remember that although individual Christians may have different attitudes to euthanasia, no Christian Church in the UK will support it. Many students get confused and say that different 'churches' have different opinions, which is not the case.

Respect for the dying

Many Christians believe that death itself is a spiritual time because the dying person is getting closer to God and preparing for the afterlife. It would therefore be wrong to interfere with this process.

Many Christians therefore support the Hospice Movement. In fact, the first modern hospice was founded by a Christian, Dame Cicely Saunders, who believed that God was asking her to help the dying in this way: Hospices:

- provide good-quality pain relief
- support the dying and those close to them
- help the dying to prepare for death.

'We are now always able to control pain in terminal cancer in the patients sent to us… euthanasia as advocated is wrong… it should be unnecessary and is an admission of defeat.' (Christian Hospice Movement)

Some Christians may still argue that euthanasia might be the most loving thing. This depends, though, on what we understand by love, and for most Christians it is to do with celebrating life, not ending it.

Summary

- Most Christians are strongly opposed to euthanasia on the grounds that life is a gift from God and no one has the right to take it away.
- Rather than encourage people to see euthanasia as an option, Christians support the Hospice Movement.

2.10 Muslim attitudes to euthanasia

Learning outcomes

By the end of this lesson, you should be able to:

● understand Muslim attitudes to euthanasia

● explain why Muslims have these different views

● give your own opinions on these different views and the reasons for them.

Activities

1 Explain in your own words why Muslims are opposed to Euthanasia.

2 Are Muslims right to oppose euthanasia? Give your views, and the reasons for them.

Muslim attitudes to euthanasia

Muslims are opposed to euthanasia because:

● They believe that all human life is sacred because it is given by Allah.

● Allah alone chooses how long each person will live and people should not interfere in this.

● It is seen as suicide which is not permitted in Islam.

● All suffering is a test, and Muslims must endure suffering without losing faith.

● No one knows Allah's plans for individuals and euthanasia would be interfering with this plan. This could have serious consequences for the afterlife.

● The Qur'an teaches: '*When their time comes they cannot delay it for a single hour nor can they bring it forward by a single hour.*' (16:61)

● The Hadith also includes a story of a person who took their own life to avoid pain of injury: '*The Prophet said: "Amongst the nations before you there was a man who got a wound, and growing impatient [with its pain], he took a knife and cut his hand with it and the blood did not stop till he died. Allah said, 'My Slave hurried to bring death upon himself so I have forbidden him (to enter) Paradise.'"*' (Sahih Bukhari 4.56.669)

● All human life is valuable whatever the circumstances and the idea of a life not worthy of living does not exist in Islam.

● It is pleasing to Allah when his people take care of the sick and old.

Allah and the nature of death

In Islam, euthanasia is thought to be as wrong as murder and suicide because people should trust their lives to Allah. Taking life would be to go against the care and protection that Allah gives to his creation. To encourage anyone to end their life is a grave sin and the Hadith warns against the consequences of suicide:

'*Whoever kills himself with an iron instrument will be carrying it forever in Hell. Whoever takes poison and kills himself will forever keep sipping that poison in Hell. Whoever jumps off a mountain and kills himself will forever keep falling down in the depths of Hell.*'

For discussion

Is it right that only Allah should be able to end a person's life?

Muslims believe that all of life is a test from Allah. If they end the test before Allah intends, they may go to *jahannam* (Hell) on the Day of Judgement.

This view is supported in the Qur'an:

'*Those who patiently persevere will truly receive a reward without measure.*' (39:10)

'*No one dies unless God permits. The term of every life is fixed.*' (3:145)

The Hadith of Sahih Bukhari supports the idea that Allah will reward those who endure pain:

'*Prophet Muhammad taught "When the believer is afflicted with pain, even that of a prick of a thorn or more, God forgives his sins, and his wrongdoings are discarded as a tree sheds off its leaves."*'

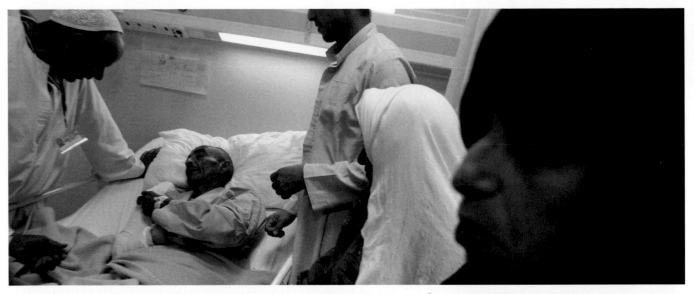

A terminally ill Muslim man is close to death and surrounded by his family.

Activities

3 List the main arguments in Islam concerning euthanasia. Which are the most convincing and which are the least convincing and why?

4 Now list the Christian points of view. In what ways are the Christian and Muslim viewpoints similar? In what ways are they different?

ResultsPlus
Watch out!

Some candidates get confused between *abortion* and *euthanasia* – make sure that you know the definition of each.

For discussion

- Should euthanasia be legalised in the UK?
- If so, under what circumstances? If not, why not?

Euthanasia and suicide

The strictest Muslim view is that all types of euthanasia are forbidden, based on the principles of *maqasid ash-Sharia'ah* (the preservation of life) and *hifdh ad-din* (the preservation of religion). This is because euthanasia allows people rather than Allah to have authority over life. And it can also encourage murder and suicide, both of which are against the principle of injury (*darar*), which demands that no one should be hurt or cause hurt to others: '*Destroy not yourselves. Surely Allah is ever merciful to you.*' (Qur'an 4:29)

Some Muslims do allow a terminal patient to choose not to continue with medical treatment if it is causing hardship and if doing so relieves the suffering of the patient and family. Some Muslims would therefore agree to the turning off of a life-support machine if nothing further can be done for the person. However, food and drink and ordinary nursing care should never be withheld while the patient is still alive.

Summary

- There is no concept of a life not worth living in Islam, and all forms of murder and suicide are forbidden. Euthanasia, therefore, is not permitted under any circumstances.
- Islam believes that suffering is to be endured as a test from Allah and many references from the Qur'an and the Hadith can be used to show that euthanasia can never be justified.
- A Muslim is not compelled to continue with medical treatment that is hopeless, but it should not be withdrawn to bring about death more quickly.

2.11 Matters of life and death in the media

Learning outcomes

At the end of this lesson, you should be able to:

- explain how different forms of the media tackle matters of life and death
- understand how the media reflect a range of different views on life-and-death issues
- offer your own opinion on how the media deal with these matters and assess how your views may be different to other people's views.

Activities

1 Have a look at a selection of this week's newspapers. Choose one or more stories to show how newspapers deal with matters of life and death.

2 In the same way, watch the television news. Explain how it deals with issues of life and death using one or more stories as examples.

3 Are there any differences between the two? Explain your answers using your examples.

It is important that matters of life and death, including abortion and euthanasia, are discussed in the media because:

- issues of life and death affect everyone
- people have very strong feelings about these issues
- opinions are very divided and it is important we are aware of different points of view
- controversial choices need to be discussed openly
- people have the right to know about developments in these issues
- people need to know how the law may change.

There are several forms of the media that allow these issues to be presented to the public:

- *Newspapers*: these have different styles of presentation and can indicate their own opinions on possible changes in the law.
- *Internet*: this makes available news and opinions, but it is often not regulated or checked for accuracy.
- *Radio*: some radio stations play features dealing with matters of life and death.
- *Television news*: daily programmes may include special features on life-and-death issues.
- *Television documentaries*: these offer the opportunity to focus on major issues at length, identifying different points of view.
- *Soap operas*: these use ongoing storylines to examine issues in depth in a way which is accessible to the general public.

- *Television dramas*: these are similar to soap operas and some may specifically focus on matters of life and death.
- *Situation comedies*: the main aim of these programmes is to make people laugh but because they take place in everyday situations and audiences can relate to the characters, these programmes often feature matters of life and death.
- *Cartoons*: like situation comedies these may deal with matters of life and death, even those aimed at children.
- *Films*: these use a detailed plot to examine an issue in depth, often based on a novel that has already introduced this idea to a smaller audience.

Soap operas

Soap operas are long-running serials concerned with everyday life in which several storylines are carried over from one episode to the next. Regular events in soap opera include issues of family and relationships, but also issues such as abortion, euthanasia, and dealing with illness and death. There is no one dominant storyline, but several stories that focus on how events affect characters are woven together over a limitless number of episodes. This means viewers can relate to the events through the familiar characters and can think about how they may respond themselves.

If a particularly emotional issue has been addressed by a soap, then a helpline phone number is often displayed at the end, so people who have been affected by the issues can get support or extra information.

Activities

4   Make a list of at least three famous TV characters who have 'died' in a programme. Describe what happened and how the programme makers handled it.

5   Do you think television soaps and other programmes handle issues of life and death well or badly? Give your reasons, using examples from television.

This photograph was taken soon after a terrorist bombing.

6   Should newspapers and television show such pictures – or should they be censored first? Give your reasons.

7   What considerations need to be taken into account before a newspaper prints a story or picture concerning a tragic death? Why?

Films and documentaries

A surprising number of films are made that tackle matters of life and death. In most cases the moral theme of a film is presented alongside the more usual themes of popular films – romance, family dramas, adventures or fantasy – because most films are designed to entertain as well as inform.

If a director simply wants to educate the audience about an issue of life or death, they will produce a documentary rather than a feature film. There are many documentaries on television that cover life-and-death issues that may not otherwise reach a wide audience. These might include issues such as rare illnesses or disabilities, or the cases of individuals who have to make difficult choices.

For discussion

• Do films and documentaries show the issues of life and death in greater detail than newspapers?

• Do you think different rules of censorship, sensitivity and good taste apply to films and documentaries, as opposed to newspapers?

Even in feature films, however, a director may deliberately choose to focus the whole film on a moral issue. Think about how they do this and whether we leave the film thinking differently about an issue. Should a director allow a one-sided view, or should they present a whole range of opinions on an issue for us to discuss and consider.

Activities

8   Write a short review of a film you have seen that dealt with matters of life and death. Give your opinion on how well or how badly the subject was treated and whether it was accurate and fair.

9   'There should be no news censorship. Television and newspapers should show things exactly as they happen.' Do you agree? Give reasons for your view.

Summary

• A wide range of media can be used to present matters of life and death to a wide audience.

• Newspapers and TV news programmes, soap operas, documentaries and films all take some responsibility for presenting issues to the public.

• Each has different intentions and interests and some may reflect the opinions of the programme makers or editors while others are more impartial.

Quick quiz

1 Which of the Ten Commandments tells us of the value of human life?

2 What is meant by 'quality of life'?

3 Why might some Christians say that it is wrong to make judgements about the quality of life?

4 According to most Muslims, when does ensoulment take place?

5 What is the latest date for an abortion, other than in exceptional cases, under UK legislation?

6 Why might a woman claim that she has a right to have an abortion?

7 Which groups of Christians are most likely to be opposed to abortion?

8 What is the 'slippery slope' argument?

9 Why might some Christians believe that suffering and illness may be valuable?

10 In what ways might non-religious people believe that life goes on beyond the grave?

Student tip

When I studied my GCSE in Religious Studies I made the mistake of thinking that all Christians or all Muslims felt the same about issues such as abortion or euthanasia. It was a surprise to me to find out that their views can be more varied than those of non-believers. You can never say 'All Christians believe ...' and be absolutely right. The most you can say is that 'Some Christians believe...' or 'Some Muslims believe...' The important thing then is explaining why they think differently, and that's the really interesting part.

Plenary activity

Find out about one person who either currently, or in recent history, has played a significant role in shaping the public's opinion on matters of life and death. For example, you could research into the life and work of Jack Kevorkian or Dianne Pretty, who carried out important work campaigning for the right for chronically sick patients to be helped to end their life. Other figures may be Joni Earekson Tada, the Christian quadriplegic, or Terry Schiavo, whose case was so controversial.

Prepare a presentation on the person you have chosen for the rest of the class, ensuring that you don't just give facts about them, but try to assess how important their case was for publicising such matters and whether you think they had any significant impact on developments in thinking about matters of life and death.

Self-evaluation checklist

Read through the following list and evaluate how well you know and understand each of the topics.
How well have you understood the topics in this section? In the first column of the table below use the following code to rate your understanding:

Green – I understand this fully
Orange – I am confident I can answer most questions on this
Red – I need to do a lot more work on this topic.

In the second and third columns you need to think about:
- Whether you have an opinion on this topic and could give reasons for that opinion if asked
- Whether you can give the opinion of someone who disagrees with you and give reasons for this alternative opinion.

Content covered	My understanding is red/orange/green	Can I give my opinion?	Can I give an alternative opinion?
Why Christians believe in life after death and how beliefs about life after death affect their lives.			
Why the followers of Islam believe in life after death and how beliefs about life after death affect their lives.			
Non-religious reasons for believing in life after death (near-death experiences, ghosts, mediums, the evidence of reincarnation).			
Why some people do not believe in life after death.			
The nature of abortion, including current British legislation, and why abortion is a controversial issue.			
Different Christian attitudes to abortion and the reasons for them.			
Different Muslim attitudes to abortion and the reasons for them.			
The nature of euthanasia, including current British legislation, and why euthanasia is a controversial issue.			
Different Christian attitudes to euthanasia and the reasons for them.			
Muslim attitudes to euthanasia and the reasons for them.			
How the media present matters of life and death.			

Find out more

For more information on the following, go to www.heinemann.co.uk/hotlinks (express code 4196P) and click on the appropriate link.

- **Life and death issues:** Christian research, education and political lobbying about life and death issues.
- **Hospice care:** This website shows the work of a famous hospice that promotes care for the dying.
- **Pregnancy advice:** British Pregnancy Advisory Service.

Introduction

In the exam you will see a choice of two questions on this section. Each question will include four tasks, which test your knowledge, understanding and evaluation of the material covered. A 2-mark question will ask you to define a term; a 4-mark question will ask you to give your opinion on a point of view; an 8-mark question will ask you to explain a particular belief or idea; a 6-mark question will ask for your opinion on a point of view and ask you to consider an alternative point of view.

Mini exam paper

(a) What is **non-voluntary euthanasia?** (2 marks)

(b) Do you agree with euthanasia?
Give **two** reasons for your point of view.

(c) Explain why some Christians do not agree with abortion. (8 marks)

(d) 'Your soul will never die.'
In your answer you should refer to at least one religion.
(i) Do you agree? Give reasons for your opinion. (3 marks)
(ii) Give reasons why some people may disagree with you. (3 marks)

You need to give a short, accurate definition. You do not need to write more than **one** clear sentence.

You need to explain the reasons why some Christians do not agree with abortion, not simply list arguments against it. This question is worth 8 marks so you must be prepared to spend some time answering it. You will also be assessed on your use of language in this question.

You must give your opinion, but make sure you do give two clear and carefully thought-out reasons. These can be ones you have learned in class, even if they are not your own opinions. You mustn't use terms such as 'rubbish' or 'stupid' as these don't show that you are able to think things through carefully.

In your answer you should state whether or not you agree with the statement. You should also give reasons for your opinion.

Now you have to give the opposite point of view, again using material you have learned during your studies. You don't have to say what you think about these alternative points of view, but you do need to show you understand why they are just as important to consider as your own opinion.

Mark scheme

(a) You can earn **2 marks** for a correct answer, and **1 mark** for a partially correct answer.

(b) To earn up to the full **4 marks** you need to give two reasons and develop them fully. Two brief reasons or only one without any development will earn **2 marks**.

(c) You can earn **7–8 marks** by giving up to four reasons, but the fewer reasons you give, the more you must develop them. Because you are being assessed on use of language, you also need to take care to express your understanding in a clear style of English, and make some use of specialist vocabulary.

(d) To go beyond **3 marks** for the whole of this question you must refer to at least one religion. The more you are able to develop your reasons the more marks you will earn. Three simple reasons can earn you the same mark as one fully developed reason.

Results Plus

Maximise your marks

(c) Explain why some Christians do not agree with abortion. (8 marks)

Student answer	Examiner comments	Improved student answer
Christians have different views on abortion but all believe that it is wrong because it violates the sanctity of life. Some Christians believe that life is so valuable that abortion can never happen.	There are some valid ideas here (such as 'sanctity of life') and the candidate has broadly understood the demands of the question, but it could be much more clearly focused with more detail given. It should focus on the Christian groups that do not agree with abortion.	Christians have different views on abortion but all believe that it is generally wrong because it violates the sanctity of life. Some Christians such as Roman Catholics and evangelical Christians believe that abortion is wrong in all situations. They believe that abortion is murder and therefore goes against one of the Ten Commandments – thou shalt not kill.
Most Christians would say that they didn't agree with abortion because it is not ever a good thing, but some would say this means that abortions should never happen, while others would say that although it is wrong it may sometimes be the lesser of two evils.	They say more about the different approaches Christians may take rather than concentrating on those Christians who say that abortion is always wrong – which is what the question is asking for. This answer would be likely to gain 4 marks.	Roman Catholics and Evangelical Christians would class abortion as murder because they believe that life begins when the baby is conceived and as all life is created by God only God has the right to take it away. They also believe that every foetus is created in God's image so this is another reason why they would always disagree with it.

Marriage and the family

Introduction

In this section you will learn about the beliefs Christians and Muslims have about marriage and the family. You will explore the role of the family and why it is important for religious believers, and the value of marriage as the foundation for that family. Religious believers often have strong views on homosexuality and contraception, and you will learn how members of the same faith may have quite different views on these issues. Non-believers as well as believers are affected, so it is important that you are aware of how society as a whole looks at the problems that these issues may raise.

Learning outcomes for this section

By the end of this section you should be able to:

- Give definitions of the key words and use them in answers to GCSE questions
- Outline the changes in attitudes in the United Kingdom to sex outside marriage, divorce, family life, and homosexuality, and give reasons for this
- Describe different Christian and Muslim attitudes to sex outside marriage, explaining why there are different attitudes
- Describe different Christian and Muslim attitudes to marriage and divorce, explaining why there are different attitudes
- Describe different Christian and Muslim attitudes to homosexuality, explaining why there are different attitudes
- Outline and explain Christian and Muslim teachings on family life and its importance
- Describe and explain different Christian and Muslim attitudes to contraception, explaining why there are different attitudes
- Explain how an issue raised in this section has been presented in the media and whether its presentation is fair to religious believers
- Express with reasons and evidence your own opinion about the issues covered in this section.

edexcel ⊞ key terms

adultery	contraception	nuclear family	promiscuity
civil partnership	faithfulness	pre-marital sex	re-constituted family
cohabitation	homosexuality	procreation	

Celebrity couple, Victoria and David Beckham.

Fascinating fact

In 2007 the provisional divorce rate in England and Wales fell to 11.9 divorcing people per 1,000 married population compared with the 2006 figure of 12.2. The divorce rate was at its lowest level since 1981. At the same time, fewer people are getting married. This is due to a number of reasons, including a decline in religious belief.

What impression of marriage do so-called 'celebrity' marriages give to young people today? Do they suggest a more or less realistic picture of married life than would be the case for the majority of people? Do 'celebrity' marriages encourage other people to adopt family values? Do you think that many media-styled 'celebrities' have considered the religious significance of their marriage? Does it matter whether they have or not? As a group, or in pairs, discuss whether you would like to get married in the future and why. Would you like to have a family? Do you think your decisions will ultimately be affected by your religion or your parents? Would you expect society's views to change more in the future and would this affect the decisions you make?

At the end of the topic, come back to your answers and see if they have been influenced by what you have learned.

3.1 Changing attitudes towards marriage, divorce, family and homosexuality in the UK

Learning outcomes

By the end of this lesson, you should be able to:

- understand and explain the changing attitudes in the UK
- outline the basic reasons for these changes
- outline some problems arising from these changes
- explain how these problems may be solved
- give your own opinion and the reasons for it.

Glossary

Divorce – The legal termination of a marriage.

Marriage – The legal union of a man and a woman.

In the UK, attitudes towards marriage, divorce, the family and **homosexuality** have changed dramatically in recent years. For example, it is now acceptable for a couple to live together without being married (**cohabitation**). The reasons for the changes in attitudes have been:

- the UK has become a multi-faith and multi-ethnic society
- people are more tolerant of the views of others
- Christian teachings are no longer taken so seriously by many people
- the Church is less influential
- reliable contraception has made sex safer
- there has been a decline in traditional family values
- women are less dependent on men for money.

edexcel key terms

Civil partnership – A legal ceremony giving a homosexual couple the same legal rights as a husband and wife.

Cohabitation – Living together without being married.

Homosexuality – Sexual attraction to people of the same sex.

Nuclear family – Mother, father and children living as a unit.

Re-constituted family – Where two sets of children (stepbrothers and stepsisters) become one family when their divorced parents marry each other.

For discussion

Is the decline of marriage a good or bad thing? Say why.

Activities

1   Describe some of the ways in which family life has changed since the 1950s.

2   **(a)** In your opinion, are there ways in which family life was better in those days than it is today?

    (b) In what ways was family life worse in those days?

A typical family photograph taken in the 1950s.

Marriage and divorce

In the UK today, fewer people are getting married than ever before. Young people, in particular, are choosing to live together (cohabitation) rather than to marry. With the decline in Church attendance, only 33 per cent of marriages are now performed as religious ceremonies.

With the significant decline in the number of people getting married, more children are being born to unmarried parents. In 1980, this was the case for 12 per cent of children, whereas today the figure is 42 per cent.

Activities

3 'Divorce rates are so high today because people no longer have a religious faith.' Would you agree? Give reasons for your view.

Families

In the twenty-first century, there are several types of family:

- **nuclear family**: two parents (man and woman) and their children all living together
- *extended family*: parents, children and other relations such as grandparents, aunts, uncles and cousins all living close to each other
- *single-parent family*: one parent living alone with their children either because the parent is unmarried or due to divorce, separation or death
- *same-sex family*: two same-sex parents and their children
- **re-constituted family**: where a man and a woman, or a same-sex couple, who have children by a previous marriage, are married and the two families have become one.

In the UK today, most people live in some sort of family set-up:

- 50 million people live in a family set-up
- 7 million people live alone
- 20 million people live in the traditional family of parents and children living together
- 18 million people are unmarried.

Homosexuality

Homosexuality is sexual attraction to members of one's own sex, as opposed to heterosexuality, which is an attraction to members of the opposite sex. In the past, homosexuality in the UK was a criminal offence but now it has become much more acceptable. The most recent change in the law was the Civil Partnerships Act of 2004 which allows same-sex partners to enter into a legally recognised commitment. Many same-sex couples choose to bring up children together.

ResultsPlus
Exam question report

Explain why there are more divorces now than there used to be. (8 marks) June 2007

How students answered

Many candidates scored poorly on this question because they explained why people get divorced rather than why more people are getting divorced now than in the past. This would receive no marks.

Most of the candidates who scored 3–4 marks for this question either offered many reasons but without explaining them, or offered one reason only, which was explained in depth.

There were a few excellent answers which suggested both practical reasons (such as 'women are no longer dependent on their husbands for money') and social or emotional reasons (such as 'UK society sees divorce as being more acceptable now').

Summary

- Attitudes to marriage, divorce, family and homosexuality have changed a great deal in recent years.
- There are different points of view about whether or not this is a good thing.

3.2 Christian attitudes to sex outside marriage

Learning outcomes

By the end of this lesson, you should be able to:

- understand and explain biblical teaching on sex outside marriage
- outline the differing views of Christians about sex outside marriage
- describe some alternative viewpoints
- explain the advantages and disadvantages of cohabitation
- give your own opinions and the reasons for them.

edexcel ⠿ key terms

Adultery – A sexual act between a married person and someone other than their marriage partner.

Faithfulness – Staying with your marriage partner and having sex only with them.

Pre-marital sex – Sex before marriage.

Promiscuity – Having sex with a number of partners without commitment.

The Bible and sexual relationships

Christianity teaches that sex outside marriage is wrong. Sex is an act of love and commitment and should only take place in marriage. This means not having sex before marriage (**pre-marital sex**) and not having sex with someone when you are already married to someone else (**adultery**). Christians are taught to avoid casual sexual relationships (**promiscuity**) and believe that married couples should show **faithfulness** to each other.

The Bible says:

'You shall not commit adultery.' (Exodus 20:14)

'God wants you to be holy and completely free from sexual immorality.' (1 Thessalonians 4:3)

'Anyone who looks at a woman lustfully has already committed adultery with her in his heart.' (Matthew 5:28)

'Do you not know that your body is a temple of the Holy Spirit?' (1 Corinthians 6:19)

'The wife's body does not belong to her alone, but also to her husband. In the same way, the husband's body does not belong to him alone but also to his wife.' (1 Corinthians 7:4)

The sexual act must take place exclusively within marriage. Outside marriage it always constitutes a grave sin. – The Catechism of the Catholic Church

Activities

1. Make a list of the quotations on this page and say what you think each of them means.
2. Do you agree or disagree with them? Give your reasons.

Different Christian opinions

Christians believe that sex outside marriage is wrong because:

- the Bible only allows sex between marriage partners
- children born outside marriage may have a less stable family life
- promiscuity makes a person vulnerable to sexually transmitted diseases
- having loving sexual relations unites a married couple
- adultery breaks the marriage vow of faithfulness.

Activities

3 Make a list of as many television programmes as you can think of that deal with sex outside marriage.

4 Do you think such programmes encourage sex outside marriage? Give your reasons.

However, a growing number of Christians today do feel that sex before marriage is right when the couple love each other, are in a long-term relationship and intend to marry each other in the future.

Indeed, many Christians today think that the teaching of the Bible and the Church on sex before marriage is old fashioned and out of touch with life in the twenty-first century. They argue that forbidding sex before marriage can cause unnecessary upset and ruin a loving relationship.

Activities

5 List the arguments for and against sex outside marriage.

6 Which arguments, in your opinion, are the most convincing, and why?

Cohabitation

Sex outside marriage is linked to the issue of cohabitation, which is when a couple live together in a sexual relationship without being married. In the UK today, about half of all couples who choose to live together do so without being married.

Some Christians believe that cohabitation helps couples to find out whether they will really be suited as marriage partners. The Church of England report called 'Something to Celebrate' said that couples who are cohabiting should be acceptable to the Church if this was a step towards marriage.

Go to www.heinemann.co.uk/hotlinks (express code 4196P) for more information on sexual abstinence.

ResultsPlus
Top tip!

Candidates who offer the best answers to questions on this topic remember that sex outside marriage covers both pre-marital and extra-marital sex. Deal with both in your answers.

Other liberal Christians (such as Methodists and Quakers) accept couples who live together into their churches. All Christians would expect couples to get married before starting a family.

Roman Catholic and evangelical Christians disagree with all sex outside marriage and therefore believe that cohabiting is wrong.

Summary

- The Bible and the Christian Church teach that sex outside marriage is wrong.
- Some Christians believe this teaching is out of date.
- Cohabitation is becoming more popular but presents its own set of problems.
- There are a range of alternative viewpoints. One example is The Silver Ring Thing.

3.3 Muslim attitudes to sex outside marriage

Learning outcomes

By the end of this lesson, you should be able to:

- understand and explain Islamic teaching on sex outside marriage
- describe the differing views of Muslims
- explain the reasons for this teaching
- describe the alternative viewpoints
- give your opinion and the reasons for it.

Glossary

Polygamy – Legally being married to more than one spouse.

Islamic teaching on sex outside marriage

For Muslims, sex outside marriage is wrong. It is strictly forbidden by the Qur'an:

'Nor come nigh to adultery for it is a shameful deed and an evil opening the road to other evils.' (Surah 17:32)

'Say to the believing men that they should lower their gaze and guard their modesty: that will make for greater purity for them: and Allah is well acquainted with all that they do.' (Surah 24:30)

In order to follow the teaching of the Qur'an:

- unmarried people must not engage in sex
- upon reaching puberty, girls and boys are often separated and do not mix with the opposite sex apart from close family members
- unmarried people must not get involved in pre-marital intimacy. ✦

It is also forbidden for Muslims to behave in a sexual manner. For example, both men and women should dress modestly and should not wear tight-fitting or revealing clothing. ✗

'And say to the believing women that they should… draw their veils over their bosoms, and not display their beauty except to their husbands' sons, their brothers or their brothers' sons, or their sisters' sons, or their womenfolk…' (Surah 24:31)

Islamic law states that sex should only take place within marriage and that the main purpose of sex is for having children. In the same way, adultery is a sin in Islam because it is forbidden by God and breaks the marriage contract. It also harms innocent family members. ✦ O

Activities

1 Make a list of the main reasons why Muslims are opposed to sex outside marriage. •

2 What are the main differences between Christian and Muslim attitudes to sex outside marriage?

3 Why is adultery a sin according to Islam?

4 Make a list of the advantages and disadvantages of not having sex outside marriage.

Selecting a marriage partner

The teachings of the Qur'an on sexual relationships outside marriage mean that committed Muslims would not choose to cohabit.

All Muslims are expected to get married. The reasons for this are:

- The Prophet Muhammad was married.
- Marriage increases the value of a person's prayers, and brings God's blessing and forgiveness.

- Sexual desire is a gift of new life from God. Men and women are encouraged, through marriage, to fulfil that desire and to have children.

Muslims in Western countries will usually choose their own marriage partners and most Muslims will marry other Muslims. Most marry at quite a young age. In some Islamic countries, Muslim men may have more than one marriage partner. This is called polygamy. This is only done under strict conditions, however, and the existing wife must give her consent to her husband taking another bride. In these Islamic countries, the maximum number of wives a man can usually have is four. However, in the UK, polygamy is illegal so Muslim men only have one wife.

65

Muslim women protesting against polygamy.

Some women in Islamic countries are against polygamy and the women in the photograph above are protesting against it.

'… *marry women of your choice, two or three or four; but if ye fear that ye shall not be able to deal justly with them, only one.*' (Surah 4:3)

For Muslims, the ideal marriage partner is one who loves God. The Prophet said: '*If someone whose faith and morals you trust makes a proposal of marriage to you, then marry him, otherwise there will be trials and much corruption in the land.*' (Hadith)

Muslims are not forced to marry particular people; parents and family may give advice but the final decision must be one which each partner freely chooses. Go to www.heinemann.co.uk/hotlinks (express code 4196P) for more information on Muslim attitudes to sex.

Summary

- The Qur'an teaches that sex outside marriage is wrong.
- Muslims should not date, be intimate or cohabit outside of marriage.
- In the West, Muslims are generally free to choose their own marriage partner.

3.4 Christian attitudes to divorce

Learning outcomes

By the end of this lesson, you should be able to:

● describe the legal position concerning divorce

● understand and explain Christian teaching on divorce

● explain the reasons for this teaching

● describe the differing views of Christians

● give your opinion and the reasons for it.

What is a divorce?

A divorce is the legal termination of a marriage. In the UK the law allows divorce if a marriage has 'irretrievably broken down'. The most common reasons for this are:

• Adultery: where one partner has sex with someone other than their marriage partner.
• Unreasonable behaviour: where one partner behaves very badly towards the other, usually over a long period of time.
• Desertion: where one partner leaves the other.

In the UK about a third of marriages end in divorce and there are about 160,000 divorces each year. People are more inclined to consider getting divorced than they were years ago, for a number of reasons:

> Divorce is easier to obtain than in the past.

> People are less willing to put up with bad treatment from their partners.

> Divorce does not carry the social stigma that it did in the past.

> People are less religious and do not feel bound to their marriage vows.

For discussion

Is it too easy to get a divorce? Should it be made more difficult?

edexcel ⠿ key terms

Re-marriage – Marrying again after being divorced from a previous marriage, or after the death of a marriage partner.

Glossary

Annulment – A declaration by the Church that a marriage never lawfully took place.

Sacrament – An outward sign of an inward blessing, as in baptism or the Eucharist.

Activities

Paul McCartney and Heather Mills had a very expensive and public divorce.

1 Do you think that when couples divorce it should be private? Give reasons for your answer.

2 Make a list of as many other celebrity divorces as you can think of.

3 'Marriage should not have to be for life.' Do you agree? Give reasons for your view.

Those in favour of divorce see it as a good provision that frees people from the need to stay in a loveless relationship. Those who are against divorce argue that it is an easy way out and that people should make a greater effort to heal the problems in their marriage.

The religious viewpoint

The Christian Church is divided over the question of divorce.

Roman Catholic Church

The Roman Catholic Church does not allow divorce because:

- Jesus said that divorce was wrong: '*Anyone who divorces his wife and marries another woman commits adultery against her.*' (Mark 10:11)
- Marriage is a sacrament and a sacred agreement (covenant) made before God that should not be broken. A Catholic who does divorce cannot **re-marry** in a Catholic Church. '*Between the baptised, a ratified and consummated marriage cannot be dissolved by any human power or for any reason other than death*' (Catechism of the Catholic Church).

For discussion

'Anyone can make a mistake – divorce should be allowed.' What do you think?

The Catholic Church will allow a couple to annul their marriage – that is, to declare that it never took place. This is possible only if it can be proved that the couple:

- did not understand what they were doing, or
- if they were forced into the marriage, or
- if the marriage was not consummated (sexual intercourse had not taken place), or
- if one of the partners was not baptised.

An annulment can only be granted with the approval of a Catholic Marriage Tribunal.

For discussion

- 'A couple who marry in church are less likely to be divorced.' Do you agree?
- What is the difference between divorce and annulment?

The Protestant Church

In the Protestant Church, divorce is allowed in certain circumstances because:

- Jesus seemed to allow for divorce in the case of unfaithfulness: '*… anyone who divorces his wife, except for marital unfaithfulness, and marries another woman commits adultery.*' (Matthew 19:9)
- People can make mistakes and relationships do break down.
- God is always ready to forgive sins.
- With God's forgiveness, believers may divorce and find happiness with a different marriage partner.

Divorced people are sometimes allowed to remarry in a Protestant Church depending on the views of the vicar.

'*Marriage should always be undertaken as a lifelong commitment but there are circumstances in which a divorced person may be married in church.*' (Church of England statement on marriage)

Activities

4 What are the main differences between the Catholic and Protestant views of divorce?

5 Which viewpoint do you support, and why?

Summary

- The Bible is not always clear on matters of divorce.
- Divorce rates are high for many different reasons.
- The Catholic Church is opposed to divorce.
- The Protestant Church allows divorce in certain circumstances.

3.5 Muslim attitudes to divorce

Learning outcomes

At the end of this lesson, you should be able to:

- understand Muslim attitudes to divorce
- explain why these attitudes are held by Muslims
- express your opinion on these attitudes and understand why people may have different opinions.

Divorce law and Islamic teaching

In the UK, the law on divorce applies to all citizens and Muslims are allowed to be legally divorced. For Muslims, marriage is a contract and contracts can be ended.

However, Islam imposes strict conditions on believers who are considering having a divorce:

- Although permitted, it is not encouraged. It is said to be among the things most disliked by Allah.
- Divorce is automatically granted if one partner leaves Islam.
- For any other reason, the husband must announce his intention to divorce his wife three times over a period of three months.
- During that time, the couple continue to live together, but do not have sexual intercourse to avoid pregnancy.
- The couple and their families have an opportunity to seek reconciliation.
- After this period is over the couple are free to remarry.
- The husband is still financially responsible for his ex-wife and their children unless she remarries.

For discussion

Why do you think that a divorce is automatically granted if a partner leaves Islam?

A man who divorces his wife must be:

- adult
- sane
- divorcing of his own free will.

Permitted grounds for divorce are very general within Islam:

'And if you fear that the two [i.e. husband and wife] may not be able to keep the limits ordered by Allah, there is no blame on either of them if she redeems herself [from the marriage tie]…' (Qur'an 2:229)

In general, the grounds on which a woman may divorce her husband include if her husband is absent for a long time without keeping in touch, long imprisonment, refusal to provide for her, or an inability to carry out sexual intercourse.

Islamic divorce

Islamic teachings on divorce are intended to discourage unpleasantness between families and to reduce unhappiness and hardship. A divorce should not be given in exchange for money and the waiting period (the *iddah*) is very important. If the wife were pregnant, then the *iddah* would last for the duration of her pregnancy and it would be wrong even to propose to a woman during her *iddah*.

The Qur'an includes strict teaching on this:

'O Prophet, when ye do divorce women, divorce them at their prescribed periods… and fear Allah your Lord; and turn them not out of the house, nor shall they leave themselves except in case they are guilty of some open lewdness…' (65:1)

If the couple are reconciled during the *iddah*, they can resume their marriage relations immediately. After the intention to divorce is announced a third time, the wife then leaves the house and is free to marry again after three months if she so wishes. She cannot marry her first husband again unless in the meantime she has married another man and been legally divorced from him following the same process.

A Muslim couple applying for a divorce.

Activities

1 Make a list of the grounds upon which a Muslim couple may divorce.

2 Outline Muslim attitudes towards divorce. Remember to include the reasons behind these attitudes.

3 List the main differences between Muslim divorce rules and Christian ones. Which are the fairest?

4 Explain the reasons why Muslims may have different views about divorce.

Islamic teaching on divorce is not designed to force unhappy couples to stay together. Instead, the process is intended to help them to find out if they can be reconciled with each other. If reconciliation is clearly impossible, the law does not create any delays or stop either partner marrying again.

Summary

- Islam permits divorce, although it is not encouraged.
- The Muslim laws on divorce are designed to help couples to be reconciled if possible.
- If they cannot be reconciled, then there are no legal obstacles to their divorce.
- The woman is protected throughout the process when the man initiates divorce.
- A woman can appeal for divorce under certain conditions.

The *iddah* does not apply to women who have entered the menopause, in which case she is free to re-marry without waiting.

Muslim community leaders will try to help couples who face divorce, by meeting and talking with them to see if there is any chance that the marriage can be saved:

'And if you fear a breach between the two, then appoint a judge from his people and a judge from her people; if they both desire agreement, Allah will effect harmony between them, surely Allah is Knowing, Aware.' (Surah 4:35)

3.6 Christian teachings on family life

Learning outcomes

By the end of this lesson, you should be able to:

● understand Christian teachings on family life

● explain why Christians hold certain beliefs about the relationships within the family

● explain how Christianity aims to help families

● give your opinion on these beliefs and justify your opinion.

The family as the foundation of society

The family is still thought to be the basis of Western society and most Christians believe that children should be brought up in a loving and supportive family. The Church should be a model of family life with members of the Church united like a family.

Most Christians believe that the best foundation for the family is marriage, and they will begin to support families by supporting couples as they prepare for marriage and by expressing their intention to support the couple throughout their married life.

For discussion

What are the main Christian beliefs concerning the family?

Christians believe that children are a gift from God, and that parents have responsibilities towards them:

● to care for them properly
● to teach them how to live and to accept authority
● to teach them about God
● to take their child to be baptised and promise to bring them up in a loving, Godly home.

In return, children are expected to respect their parents and to obey them until they are adults themselves.

Husband and wife, parents and children

'*Marriage is given, that husband and wife may comfort and help each other, living faithfully together in need and in plenty, in sorrow and in joy… it is given that they may have children and be blessed in caring for them and bringing them up in accordance with God's will.*' (Church of England Prayer Book)

The Bible teaches that children should '*Honour your father and your mother*' (Exodus 20:12). Looking at the relationship between parents and children, it teaches: '*Children, obey your parents… Parents, do not exasperate your children; instead, bring them up in the instruction of the Lord*' (Ephesians 6:1,4).

Activities

A Christian family.

1 What is the family in the photograph doing and why?

2 What would you include in a set of guidelines for bringing up a child? Remember that you have to cater for the child's emotional and spiritual needs as well as physical ones.

3 What are the main guidelines that a Christian parent should follow when bringing up children?

4 What are the main guidelines that a child should follow when being brought up by Christian parents?

The importance of the family is underlined by this statement by the Roman Catholic Church:

'The family is the community in which, from childhood, one can learn moral values, begin to honour God and make good use of freedom' (Catechism of the Catholic Church).

For discussion

What does 'Honour your father and your mother' mean?

Christians believe that all children have the right to be brought up in a loving family setting, so some Christians work with charities involved with family life, including the Children's Society and the National Children's Homes.

The social environment of the Church

Christian Churches try to help parents to raise their children in a stable, Christian environment, taking pressure off them when necessary and helping them to stay together in a happy unit.

This starts at the beginning of life, when parents bring babies to church for an infant baptism, or dedicate the children to God at a service of dedication and promise to bring them up in a loving Christian home. Older children can re-affirm these baptismal vows for themselves in a believer's baptism or confirmation.

As children grow up, they may attend Sunday Schools and youth groups where young people can learn about God in a social environment. Church schools educate children in a Christian environment and many Christian parents choose to send their children to a Church or faith school rather than a community school.

For discussion

Why do you think Christian parents may want to send their children to a Church school?

Churches also hold family services on Sundays and special services at Christmas, Easter and Harvest festival. They may also help in the running of such organisations as the Scouts and the Brownies. Many churches will have a time in the weekly service which is targeted at the children, and in which they may participate.

Activities

5   List the ways in which the Church can help to support Christian families.

6   Explain why family life is so important for Christians.

Help and support from the Church

Christian Churches also offer help and advice to families through counselling and the running of such organisations as the Catholic Marriage Advisory Council and the Child Welfare Council. Churches may help Christian adults to look after their elderly parents through such organisations as the Methodist Homes for the Aged.

'Grown children have responsibilities towards their parents. As much as they can, they must give them moral support in old age and in times of illness, loneliness or distress.' (Catechism of the Catholic Church)

Summary

- Christians see the family as very important for bringing up children so that they know what is good.
- Parents should take responsibility for teaching their children and children should respect their parents.
- Christian churches offer parents support in bringing up their family and encouraging children to become Christians.

3.7 Muslim teachings on family life

Lesson outcomes

By the end of this lesson, you should be able to:

- explain Muslim teachings on family life
- understand why they are important to Islam and for being a Muslim
- express your opinion on these teachings and assess how they differ from the opinions of others.

The heart of the community

Within Islam, the family is at the heart of the Muslim community. It is also the most important way of ensuring that children grow up as good faithful Muslims.

- There are plenty of opportunities for religious activities at home as well as in the mosque.
- Parents are responsible for the religious upbringing of their children. The mother is at the heart of the Muslim family. In a traditional family the mother is responsible for teaching the children about *halal* and *haram* in the home while the father is responsible for taking the boys to the mosque.
- The beliefs and values of Islam, including the principles of *haram* (forbidden) and *halal* (permitted), are learned first in the family.

- Parents have the responsibility to send their children to the *madrasah*, where Muslim children can learn to read the Qur'an in Arabic.
- Some Muslim parents in the UK may choose to send their children to Muslim schools.
- Within the mosque, the *imam* may offer advice on all matters of marriage and family life.
- Financial aid may be given to families from the *zakah* fund in times of need.

Activities

1 Outline the main Muslim teachings concerning family life.

2 Explain how these teachings enable children to grow up to be faithful Muslims.

3 *Role-play*. You are a Muslim teenager and your friend is Christian teenager. Explain to each other how your family lives differ.

A Muslim family celebrating Ramadan together.

Family values

Islam teaches that the values of family life are so important and so long-lasting that they are the foundation of society. Family values are based on the Qur'an and traditions from the life and teaching of Muhammad and are handed down thorough the generations.

Family life is the cradle of human society providing a secure, healthy and encouraging environment for parents and growing children.

For discussion

Do religious guidelines help or hinder family life? Give your reasons.

- Family life is the arena in which human virtues such as love, kindness, mercy and compassion can be developed.
- Family life is the most secure protection against troubles in society and within the individual.
- Family life encourages the individual to see themselves as part of a wider community and discourages anti-social behaviour.
- Muslims believe that these values are not just for the benefit of individual families, but also the worldwide family (*ummah*) of Islam. The family group and the *ummah* are kept together in three ways: kinship (blood ties), marriage and faith. These are seen to be in the order of most importance, but sometimes faith will take first place if there is a conflict of interests.

Activities

4 Make a list of the main responsibilities held by: **(a)** a Muslim parent; and **(b)** a Muslim child.

5 Do Muslim guidelines make family life easier or harder for: **(a)** parents; and **(b)** children? Explain your reasons.

The traditional Muslim family

The traditional Muslim family is an extended one: it includes not only parents and children, but also grandparents and elderly relatives. Muslims believe that extended families mean greater stability, continuity, love and support for each other.

The elderly are treated with dignity. Muslims consider it to be an honour and a blessing from God to be able to look after elderly relatives. After all, it was the now-elderly grandparents who looked after the next generation when they were children. For Muslims, looking after elderly members of the family is a sacred action, which should be done with kindness, patience and respect. The Qur'an states:

'*Your Lord has commanded that you worship none but Him and that you be kind to your parents. If one of them or both of them reach old age with you, do not say to them a word of disrespect… and act humbly to them in mercy.*' (Surah 17:23–24)

Activities

6 What are the advantages and disadvantages of living in an extended family?

7 What do you think it means to treat the elderly with respect?

Summary

- The family is at the heart of the Muslim community and the place where children grow up to be good Muslims and understand the importance of Islam as a way of life.
- Parents and children have important responsibilities within the family.
- The family is the way in which Muslim life is best protected.
- Marriage is the key to the family and all Muslims are expected to marry.

3.8 Christian attitudes to homosexuality

Learning outcomes

By the end of this lesson, you should be able to:

- understand different Christian attitudes to homosexuality
- explain why Christians hold different opinions
- express your own opinion and explain why other people have different views.

edexcel ⠿ key terms

Civil partnership – A legal ceremony giving a homosexual couple the same legal rights as a husband and wife.

Glossary

Celibacy – Refraining from sexual activity for religious reasons.

Opposition to homosexuality

Although attitudes to homosexuality have changed in society, many religious believers still claim it is against Christian teaching because:

- God created man and woman to be in a marriage relationship together.
- Two same-sex partners cannot have a child through natural sexual intercourse.
- Homosexuality is not good for society, as it undermines the family.
- The Bible teaches against homosexuality: *'Do not lie with a man as one lies with a woman; that is detestable'* (Leviticus 18:22).
- In the New Testament Paul writes *'Neither the sexually immoral… nor homosexual offenders… will inherit the Kingdom of God'* (1 Corinthians 6:9–10).

Most evangelical, conservative Christians are strongly opposed to homosexuality and in some cases will not allow known homosexuals to be members of their churches. The Roman Catholic Church recommends that homosexuals remain celibate (do not have active sexual relationships).

Other Christians, however, such as the Lesbian and Gay Christian Movement, argue that homosexuality is a perfectly natural state of being and that homosexuals are born (or created by God) as homosexuals. A few Churches will give a blessing to a same-sex partnership.

Activities

1. What is homosexuality?
2. Outline UK law regarding homosexuality.
3. What is a civil partnership?
4. How is a civil partnership different from a marriage?

Greater tolerance for homosexuality

In the Church of England and other more liberal Protestant Churches, the approach toward homosexuals is more sympathetic and there is a very strong Gay Christian Movement. In this case, homosexual partnerships are judged on the strength of the love and commitment of the partners rather than simply rejecting them as wrong:

*In 2005, gay singer Elton John entered into a **civil partnership** with his long-term partner, David Furnish.*

'There are circumstances in which individuals may justifiably choose to enter into a homosexual relationship with the hope of enjoying companionship and a physical expression of love similar to that found in marriage.' (Church of England Statement on Sexuality)

For discussion

Do the views of the Church of England and liberal Protestant Churches support or oppose the teachings in the Bible?

Although in the Church of England, celibate homosexuals may become priests, some congregations will still not accept a homosexual priest in their church, and it is a matter which causes great division. In 2003, Bishop Jeffrey John was not appointed Bishop of Reading because of the controversy over his homosexuality, although in the US the Reverend Gene Robinson was appointed Bishop in New England, despite many people still being opposed to his appointment.

For discussion

Why are Christians so divided in their views of homosexuality?

ResultsPlus
Top tip!

Candidates who use adjectives such as 'most', 'many', and 'some' when describing the beliefs of different religious believers (for example 'Many Christians believe…') will receive better marks. Those who generalise and say all members of a religion think something receive no marks.

Activities

5 How do different Churches view the appointment of gay priests? Who do you most agree with, and why?

The range of Christian views on homosexuality

- 'Homosexuality is a disorder from which the Christian can seek God's help.' This is the most conservative Christian attitude.
- 'Homosexual relationships should be celibate.' This is a less conservative Christian attitude and accepts that homosexuality is a natural state for some, but should not be practised.
- 'Whilst exclusive homosexual relationships are not ideal, they are better than promiscuity.' This is moving towards a liberal Christian position.
- 'The Church should fully accept homosexual partnerships and welcome homosexuals into the priesthood.' This is a fully liberal Christian attitude, accepting homosexuality as equally valid as heterosexuality.

Summary

- Most Christians are opposed to homosexuality on the grounds that the Bible teaches against it and that it is not a natural state for human reproductive relationships.
- Although the law is more accepting of homosexual relationships, the Churches are divided, especially in the case of homosexual clergy.
- Some conservative Christian groups preach actively against homosexuality.
- More liberal groups allow that it may be natural and should be accepted to some degree.

3.9 Muslim attitudes to homosexuality

Learning outcomes

At the end of this lesson, you should be able to:

- understand different Muslim attitudes to homosexuality
- explain the reasons for these different attitudes
- give your opinion and express reasons for it
- understand why people may disagree with your opinion.

Activities

1 Why is homosexuality punishable by death in some Muslim countries?

Strongly against homosexuality

Islam takes a very strong position regarding homosexuality:

- It is seen as a grave sin.
- Under Shari'ah law it is punishable by death.
- One Hadith of the Prophet goes as far as saying,

  'Kill the one that is doing it and also kill the one that it is being done to.'

- Al-Fatiha, a Muslim homosexual rights group, estimates that more than 4,000 homosexuals have been executed in Iran since 1979 while 10 public executions of homosexuals have been performed by the Taliban army in Afghanistan.

  'What! Of all creatures do ye come unto the males, and leave the wives your Lord created for you? Nay, but ye are forward folk.' (Qur'an 26:165)

- It is thought to be harmful to the health of the individuals.

Homosexuality is seen as a serious challenge to the Muslim laws against effeminacy in men and masculine characteristics in women.

For discussion

Why is homosexuality regarded as so harmful by Muslims?

In the Qur'an, the story of the 'people of Lot', who are also known as the Sodomites, tells how they were destroyed by Allah because they practised homosexuality. This has been the basis for it being forbidden in Islam, although punishments vary. Some Islamic legal traditions prescribe the death penalty, but in some Islamic countries punishments are milder and may not be imposed at all.

Same-sex intercourse officially carries the death penalty in several Muslim states including Saudi Arabia, Iran, northern Nigeria and Sudan, and formerly in Afghanistan under the Taliban. In some nations where there are a majority of Muslims such as Turkey and Jordan, same-sex intercourse is not specifically forbidden by law. Iran is probably the nation to execute the largest number of its citizens for homosexuality.

Although human rights groups such as Amnesty International condemn laws which make consenting homosexual acts a crime, most Muslim nations (apart from those in the EU, such as Turkey) insist that anti-homosexual laws, based on the Qur'an, are necessary to preserve Islamic behaviour and morality.

Support for homosexuals is controversial

Islam sees homosexuality as a threat to the stability of Islamic society, which is based around the family and, naturally, reduces the number of children to be born into Islam. However, some modern Muslims controversially offer support to homosexual Muslims, rather than let them be excluded from the community. There is an online community for homosexual Muslims who are afraid to come out as homosexual within the Muslim community.

Traditionally, however, Islam teaches that homosexuality is a chosen, not natural, sexual orientation, and that any homosexual can become heterosexual if they are educated towards it.

For discussion

Is homosexuality chosen or natural? Give your view, with reasons.

The Al-Fatiha Foundation accepts homosexuality as natural and suggests that the teaching of the Qur'an is no longer relevant to the modern world. It also draws attention to the fact that the Qur'an condemns homosexual lust but not love (much as the New Testament does). Within the Shi'ah school of thought in Islam, thinkers such as Ayatollah Khomeini have argued in favour of a sex change operation for some men who are homosexual.

Activities

2 Compare Christian and Muslim attitudes towards homosexuality.

3 Explain the reasons why Muslims are divided over homosexuality.

Discussion in the media

Modern approaches to the issue of homosexuality within Islam are now more publically presented. In the 2007 documentary film, *Jihad for Love*, the director interviewed gay Muslims from all around the world, many of whom had to remain anonymous because of fear of reprisals. He had found many of his contacts online and he received thousands of emails from people who had heard of his work. Most were supportive, but he reported that he had also received many hate emails.

In 2006, Channel 4 also produced a documentary called *Gay Muslims* which addressed the tensions for a homosexual Muslim in a world in which social views are changing but Muslim law in many countries is seen as unchangeable.

A gay Muslim protest march in London in support of the Al-Fatiha Foundation.

For many Muslims, laws against homosexuality cannot change and the concept of a 'gay Muslim' is seen as impossible and contradicts the meaning of being a Muslim. Islam means submission to the will of Allah, and if Allah's law opposes homosexuality then it is not possible to be gay and be a follower of Islam. Go to www.heinemann.co.uk/hotlinks (express code 4196P) for more information on Muslim attitudes to homosexuality.

Summary

- Most Muslims are strongly opposed to homosexuality because it is against the teachings of the Qur'an and Islamic law.

- Some Muslim countries prescribe the death penalty for homosexuality, others are now more lenient, and some have decriminalised it.

- The problems of being a gay Muslim are now discussed in the media but there are still many Muslims who claim that it is impossible to be gay and a Muslim.

3.10 Christian attitudes to contraception

Learning outcomes

By the end of this lesson, you should be able to:

● explain why some people use contraception

● explain different Christian positions on contraception

● understand why they hold different attitudes

● give your opinion on these different attitudes and understand why some people may have different views.

Reasons for preventing pregnancy

Contraception is the deliberate prevention of pregnancy by natural or artificial methods.

People who use contraception usually do so because they have decided that it is not appropriate for them to have children. This may be because:

- They want to plan when to have their family.
- They consider themselves too young or too old.
- They do not believe they would be good parents.
- Becoming pregnant would be harmful to the health of the mother.
- One or both partners carry a genetically inherited condition.
- They feel they could not provide financially or emotionally for a child.
- They have a lifestyle they feel would not be compatible with having a child.
- In the case of a single man, he does not want to be responsible for a woman's pregnancy.

Religious opposition to using contraception

Many people use contraception at some point in their lives but some religious believers are opposed to it. Roman Catholics and some conservative evangelicals believe that every act of sexual intercourse should be open to the possibility of conception.

edexcel ▦ key terms

Contraception – Intentionally preventing pregnancy from occurring.

Activities

Vicky Pollard in a comic scene from Little Britain.

1 Describe what the photograph shows. Say what you think about the situation shown.

2 Explain the reasons why someone might choose not to use contraception.

They argue that using artificial methods of contraception is wrong because:

- They prevent people fulfilling God's command to '*Be fruitful and multiply*' (Genesis 1:28).
- The purpose of marriage is to have children.
- Sex was given by God for procreation and so should always allow for the possibility of conception.
- Contraception has allowed promiscuity and promiscuity spreads sexually transmitted diseases.

Therefore, some Christians believe they should only use a natural method of contraception, planning their love-making around the woman's menstrual cycle, and attempting to predict the times in the cycle when she is not likely to conceive.

Many Catholics themselves disagree with this official teaching of the Roman Catholic Church on contraception, particularly those in countries which are affected with a high level of AIDS.

For discussion

Should sexual intercourse always be open to the possibility of pregnancy?

Activities

3 Explain the reasons why Christians disagree on contraception.

4 'It is better to use contraception than to have an unwanted baby.' Do you agree? Give reasons for your view.

Results Plus
Watch out!

Always read the question really carefully in the exam. The words 'conception' and 'contraception' mean very different things, so if you misread the question you may get no marks at all for your answer!

Other Christian views

The Church of England has stated that it does not regard contraception as a sin or a contravention of God's purpose, although some members would suggest that a couple who had never allowed for the possibility of having children at any point in their marriage were in some way missing out on God's best intentions for people.

Other Christians, however, consider that within a marriage relationship, contraception can be used properly to plan and manage a family. Although children are seen as a blessing from God, Christians should still have a responsible attitude to conception, particularly in cases of financial need or ill health.

For most, a barrier method such as the cap or condom is acceptable, since the sperm and egg are prevented from meeting and so conception cannot take place. For many Christians, however, the coil and the morning-after pill, which act after conception, and prevent implantation, are considered to be the equivalent of an abortion and are therefore unacceptable. The conventional pill, which prevents conception, is acceptable.

For discussion

- Is having ten or more children God's will or irresponsible?
- Do we have the right to control birth by using contraception?

Summary

- Most Christians today accept some form of contraception as a responsible way of planning a family.
- Most will also see children as a blessing from God but will allow that this does not mean having an unlimited number of children.
- Roman Catholic teaching holds that only a natural method of contraception is permissible, although more Catholics are now challenging this view.

3.11 Muslim attitudes to contraception

Learning outcomes

At the end of this lesson, you should be able to:

- explain why some people use contraception
- explain different Muslim positions on contraception
- understand why they hold different attitudes
- give your opinion on these different attitudes and understand why some people may have different views.

edexcel ::: key term:

Procreation – Making a new life.

A range of viewpoints

Within Islam, there are mixed views on contraception:

- Some Muslims are completely opposed to contraception.
- Others maintain that it is permissible if the mother's life or health would be in danger if she became pregnant.
- Some believe that if the family – existing children, or the new child – would suffer materially or physically, then its use is justifiable.
- Contraception should therefore not be considered as serious as abortion and it is not open to the same criticism.

Activities

1 Why do you think that some Muslims are completely opposed to contraception?

Islamic teaching about the family is very strong and regards it as the ideal environment for growing up as a Muslim, so children are always seen as a gift from God. Muslim sexual ethics forbid sex outside marriage, so its teachings about contraception are all concerned with the relationship between husband and wife. Contraception can never be justified in the case of unmarried or adulterous partners.

For discussion

Is the Christian view of contraception more or less strict than the Muslim view? Why?

Conservative opposition

The most conservative Islamic leaders have openly challenged the use of condoms or other artificial birth control methods, which means that family planning through artificial methods of contraception is impossible in strict Muslim countries. Although some Islamic medical professionals are in favour of promoting contraception for married couples, they cannot make an official statement in support of it.

There is no specific reference to contraception in the Qur'an, but Muslims opposed to it refer to the text '*You should not kill your children for fear of want*' (17:31, 6:151) although this is commonly used to oppose abortion. Supporters of contraception argue that this interpretation is not what was originally intended by the text.

Situations and types of contraception that are acceptable

In reality, most Muslim authorities allow contraception to preserve the health of the mother or the well-being of the family, not least because there are several Hadith which suggest that the Prophet knew of the withdrawal method of birth control and approved of it in certain circumstances.

The withdrawal method is, however, very unreliable, and cannot guarantee that conception will not still take place. Furthermore, some Muslims feel that because it may prevent the woman having sexual fulfilment and deprive her of having children, that her consent must first be obtained.

Activities

Muslim women in India protesting against the use of contraception.

2 Why do you think the people in the photograph are protesting?

3 What do you think the text *'You should not kill your children for fear of want'* really means?

4 Should contraception only be available to married couples?

Some Muslim thinkers have argued that any method that has the same purpose as withdrawal is acceptable, so long as it does not have a permanent effect. In this case sterilisation and vasectomy would be forbidden.

It is permissible to use condoms so long as this does not cause any harm and so long as both husband and wife consent to their use, because this is similar to 'azl (*coitus interruptus* or withdrawal).

For discussion

- Does contraception encourage promiscuity?
- Why are Muslims divided in their views on contraception?

Contraceptive methods that do not prevent conception but cause a very early abortion are not accepted and neither is the use of contraception if it is to ensure that a married couple never have children at any stage in their marriage. Muslims believe that **procreation** within the family is a religious duty, so use of contraception must always be considered seriously, and only if it is for the genuine well-being of the couple or the rest of the family.

Interestingly, in some Shi'ah Muslim countries, contraception is taught to young couples through posters and advertisements, for economic reasons as well as to protect the mother. Some Muslims believe that contraception makes a woman more attractive to her husband throughout their married life, and for some Muslim women, the freedom to use contraception frees them from male domination.

The Islamic faith allows a lot of flexibility in the interpretation of teachings on contraception. This is reflected in the different family planning policies used by different Muslim groups (even when in the same country).

Summary

- Muslim teaching on contraception is very flexible, and although some Muslim states prohibit it, some actively teach it to young people.
- When there are good reasons, which protect the family and the married couple, it is permitted.
- Contraception is never permitted if it is to encourage promiscuity or an illicit relationship.

examzone

Know Zone
Marriage and the family

Quick quiz

1 What is the Muslim attitude to sex outside of marriage?

2 What is 'adultery'?

3 Which groups of Christians are opposed to the use of contraception?

4 Name two forms of artificial contraception.

5 How many times must a Muslim man announce his intention to divorce his wife?

6 Why do many Christians oppose divorce?

7 Why does the Bible highlight the importance of the family?

8 What does 'civil partnership' mean?

9 How is the Church a model of the family unit?

10 In what ways might a religious belief keep a family together?

Student tip

When I studied GCSE Religious Studies, I found this topic the hardest to appreciate as I felt that it presented a misleading picture of marriage and family in society today. It seemed that it simply wasn't realistic, because no one I knew was in a religious family and I felt the attitudes of some religious people to issues such as homosexuality to be unacceptable.

It wasn't until I visited one of my friends, who is a Muslim, that I saw some people do take religion seriously and it does influence the way they live. Although it wouldn't suit me, it made me understand that there are good reasons for some people to live that way.

Plenary activity

As a group, or in pairs, discuss how families are presented in popular television programmes. Take responsibility for looking at one programme per pair in each small group and report your findings and opinions back to the class.

Overall did you find that families in soap operas and popular dramas are presented as typical of families you know, even your own family, or as very different? Are they true to life? How do they deal with problems that arise in the family, such as opposition to a homosexual member of the family, or divisions over whether to have children or not?

Do any families in soap operas appear to be influenced in their lifestyle by religion? If so are they presented as a stereotype or do they appear more true to life? How far does what you have learned in this topic help you to understand these families better or are they just too different to compare?

Self-evaluation checklist

Read through the following list and evaluate how well you know and understand each of the topics.
How well have you understood the topics in this section? In the first column of the table below use the following code to rate your understanding:

Green – I understand this fully
Orange – I am confident I can answer most questions on this
Red – I need to do a lot more work on this topic.

In the second and third columns you need to think about:

- Whether you have an opinion on this topic and could give reasons for that opinion if asked
- Whether you can give the opinion of someone who disagrees with you and give reasons for this alternative opinion.

Content covered	My understanding is red/orange/ green	Can I give my opinion?	Can I give an alternative opinion?
● Changing attitudes to marriage, divorce, family life, homosexuality and contraception in the UK and the reasons for them.			
● Christian attitudes to sex outside marriage and the reasons for them.			
● Muslim attitudes to sex outside marriage and the reasons for them.			
● Different Christian attitudes to divorce, and the reasons for them.			
● Different Muslim attitudes to divorce and the reasons for them.			
● Christian teachings on family life and its importance.			
● Muslim teachings on family life and its importance.			
● Different Christian attitudes to homosexuality and the reason for them.			
● Muslim attitudes to homosexuality and the reasons for them.			
● Different Christian attitudes to contraception and the reasons for them.			
● Different Muslim attitudes to contraception and the reasons for them.			

Find out more

For more information on the following, go to www.heinemann.co.uk/hotlinks (express code 4196P) and click on the appropriate link.

- **Christian guidance:** Guidance for Christian couples seeking to accept as many children as God gives them.
- **Gay support:** Support for gay and lesbian Muslims.
- **Roman Catholic guidance**: Information on Roman Catholic positions on all matters of interest to Catholics.
- **Family:** Evangelical Christian teaching on the role of the family today.
- **Gay support online:** Online support for gay Muslims.
- **Silver Ring Thing:** An organisation supporting young people who wish to wait until they are married before having sex.
- **Muslim attitudes to sex:** For further information on Muslim attitudes.

exam zone

Know Zone
Marriage and the family

Introduction

In the exam you will see a choice of two questions on this section. Each question will include four tasks which test your knowledge, understanding and evaluation of the material covered. A 2-mark question will ask you to define a term; a 4-mark question will ask your opinion on a point of view; an 8-mark question will ask you to explain a particular belief or idea; a 6-mark question will ask for your opinion on a point of view and ask you to consider an alternative point of view.

You can give your opinion, but make sure you do give two clear and carefully thought-out reasons. These can be ones you have learned in class, even if they are not your own opinion. You mustn't use terms such as 'rubbish' or 'stupid' as these don't show that you are able to think things through carefully.

Mini exam paper

(a) What is **cohabitation?**
(2 marks)

Here you need to give a short, accurate definition. You do not need to write more than **one** clear sentence.

(b) Do you think divorce is better than an unhappy marriage?
Give **two** reasons for your point of view. (4 marks)

(c) Choose **one** religion other than Christianity and explain why most of the followers of that religion are against sex outside marriage. (8 marks)

Here you need to explain the reasons why most followers of that faith are against sex outside marriage and not simply list their reasons. This question is worth 8 marks so you must be prepared to spend some time answering it. You will also be assessed on your use of language in this question.

(d) 'No religious person should be homosexual.'
In your answer you should refer to at least one religion.
(i) Do you agree? Give reasons for your opinion. (3 marks)
(ii) Give reasons why some people may disagree with you. (3 marks)

In your answer you should state whether or not you agree with the statement. You should also give reasons for your opinion.

Now you have to give the opposite point of view, again, using material you have learned during your studies. You don't have to say what you think about these alternative points of view, but you do need to show you understand why they are just as important to consider as your own opinion.

Mark scheme

(a) You can earn **2 marks** for a correct answer, and **1 mark** for a partially correct answer.

(b) To earn up to the full **4 marks** you need to give two reasons (as asked) and to develop them fully. Two brief reasons or only one without any development will earn **2 marks.**

(c) You can earn **7–8 marks** by giving up to four reasons, but the fewer reasons you give, the more you must develop them. You are being assessed on your use of language so you also need to take care to express your understanding in a clear style of English, and make some use of specialist vocabulary.

(d) To go beyond **3 marks** for the whole of this question you must refer to at least one religion. The more you are able to develop your reasons the more marks you will earn. Three simple reasons can earn you the same mark as one fully developed reason.

ResultsPlus

Maximise your marks

(d) 'No religious person should be homosexual.'
In your answer you should refer to at least one religion.
(i) Do you agree? Give reasons for your opinion. (3 marks)
(ii) Give reasons why some people may disagree with you. (3 marks)

Student answer	Examiner comments	Improved student answer
i) I disagree with the claim that no religious person should be homosexual because this is an unloving approach. Some people will be homosexual because they are naturally that way and there is no point using religious teaching against them as this is unkind.	The candidate has clearly given their opinion and a reason for it. This will gain two marks as the candidate has only developed one idea.	i) I disagree with the claim that no religious person should be homosexual because this is an unloving approach, and Jesus taught that we should love people whoever they are. Some people will be homosexual because they arc naturally that way and there is no point using religious teaching against them as this is unkind. Many liberal Christians would agree with me and there are many gay Christians who would also share my opinion.
ii) Some people may disagree because they do not believe that homosexuality is natural and that if the teachings of their religion are against it, then they must obey those teachings, whether it feels right for them or not.	This answer is very simple and does not describe the religious teachings mentioned and why they may be used by some believers to take the opposite view.	ii) Some people may disagree because there are teachings in the Bible which are against homosexuality. Many evangelical Christians would disagree with me for this reason and because they believe that the purpose of sex is to have children, which is not possible for a homosexual couple.

Religion and community cohesion

Introduction

This section covers the issues that arise within the United Kingdom as a multi-ethnic and multi-faith nation. In it, you will learn about what Christians and Muslims believe about gender roles, racism, prejudice and discrimination. You will learn how Christians and Muslims work to promote racial harmony and community cohesion, so that all people in the UK can live peacefully and happily together. You will also gain an understanding of the problems that arise and why racism and other controversial attitudes remain.

Learning outcomes for this section

By the end of this section you should be able to:

- Give definitions of the key words and use them in answers to GCSE questions
- Outline changing attitudes to gender roles in the United Kingdom
- Describe different Christian and Muslim attitudes to equal rights for women, explaining why there are different attitudes
- Understand that the United Kingdom is a multi-faith and multi-ethnic society
- Express your own opinions on racism and discrimination in the United Kingdom today
- Outline and explain why Christians and Muslims should promote racial harmony
- Describe government action to promote community cohesion in the United Kingdom
- Describe ways in which religions work to promote community cohesion in the United Kingdom
- Explain how an issue raised in this section has been presented in the media and whether its presentation is fair to religious believers
- Express with reasons and evidence your own opinion about the issues covered in this section.

edexcel ⠿ key terms

community cohesion	interfaith marriages	prejudice	religious freedom
discrimination	multi-ethnic society	racial harmony	religious pluralism
ethnic minority	multi-faith society	racism	sexism

OMMUNITY COHESION
EBSITE FOR THE WHOLE SCHOOL COMMUNITY

EWEB helps you easily create a school website that can engage and involve the community – children, families, staff, governors and the wider community. It's one big step towards community cohesion.

This poster promotes community cohesion. Within the UK, as elsewhere, it is important that people of different races and religious faiths live peacefully alongside one another. In many areas, there has been great success, but in other areas this has not always been the case and there is still a long way to go.

Take a sheet of A3 paper, turn it landscape, and write RELIGION & COMMUNITY COHESION in the middle of it. As a class, or in groups or pairs, make a list or a chart outlining all the positive advantages that being a member of a multi-faith and multi-ethnic society can bring. Then list the disadvantages. Finally, look at both lists and see which one, in your opinion, has the best and most convincing reasons, and explain why.

For example, you could start with an advantage: *understanding each other* (Christians understanding the views of Muslims and vice versa). Then consider one of the disadvantages: *problems of racism* (believing that one race is superior to another). And conclude with a positive action that might emerge from this situation, for example, *attempts to encourage community cohesion* (activities directed towards helping people to live in harmony together).

When you have finished studying this section you can turn back to this sheet and see if you want to add, change or take away any of the points you have listed. Then decide how successful attempts at community cohesion have been and consider what else could be done.

Fascinating fact

Of the UK population, 92 per cent are white British and only 8 per cent are from other racial groups.

Bowes Primary School Community Centre

4.1 Changing attitudes to gender roles in the UK

Learning outcomes

By the end of this lesson, you should be able to:

- describe the changing roles of women in the UK
- explain what is meant by 'women's rights'
- describe some of the ways in which the roles of men are changing
- express your own opinions about gender roles
- explain the inequalities that remain.

edexcel ::: key terms

Discrimination – Treating people less favourably because of their ethnicity, gender, colour, sexuality, age or class.

Prejudice – The belief that some people are inferior or superior without even knowing them.

Sexism – Discrimination against people because of their gender (being male or female).

Glossary

Equality – The state of everyone having equal rights regardless of their gender, race or class.

For discussion

Although men and women have equal rights, why do you think that most of the people in the top jobs are men?

Changing roles

Until the middle of the twentieth century, most people thought that a woman's role in society was to stay at home and look after the children. It was only in 1918 that women were allowed to vote and it was not until 1970 that women were given a right to receive equal pay (when doing the same job as a man). Women's roles in society have dramatically changed along with their legal rights. Now, in the twenty-first century, women have completely different lives. However, are they *really* treated as being equal with men?

In recent years, the traditional roles of men have changed significantly too. Many men take a much more active role in the raising of children and the care of the home. Men are much more willing to cook and do the tasks which used to be seen as 'women's work'. At the extreme, there are even transsexuals (such as Thomas Beatie) who are becoming pregnant.

Making progress

A century ago only 15 per cent of married women worked outside the home. However, during the two World Wars, attitudes changed because women had to do the work of men who had gone to fight in the wars. After each war ended, women's organisations campaigned for equal rights for women.

There was, however, resistance. Many people believed that men *should* earn more money than women, because they had families to support, and also that children were looked after best if raised by a mother who did not go to work.

Today, in the UK, legally women and men have equal rights. Nevertheless, inequalities still exist. For instance, recent surveys have shown that rates of pay for men and women are still not equal and men can earn around 17 per cent more. Also, the traditional

Activities

1 In 2008, on the Oprah Winfrey show, Thomas Beatie, a transsexual, said: 'I'm a person and I have the right to have my own biological child.' Do you agree?

2 What do you think about Thomas Beatie's pregnancy?

Activities

3   Make a list of the traditional roles for men and women in the UK. This has been started for you in the table below. Do you think these present problems today?

Traditional men's roles	Traditional women's roles
Going out to work	Bringing up children

4   What example of gender and/or **sexist** stereotypes can you name in the media (perhaps in advertisements or in films such as 'chick flicks')? Are they offensive?

5   Can you name any jobs you think should only be done by *either* men *or* women, but not by both?

roles do still exist, with women doing the majority of household chores and childcare. In the workplace there are still jobs that are seen as 'female' (for example, nursing), and there are far fewer women than men in positions of real power. There are also still many instances of **discrimination** and **prejudice** against women.

A board of directors of a company. How much do you think attitudes towards women have changed in business in recent years? How many business leaders can you name who are women?

ResultsPlus
Top tip!

⚠   The best answers to questions on this topic focus on the changes that have taken place in the UK and how they have affected attitudes to gender roles.

Breaking through

In the early twenty-first century, there are more examples than ever before of women achieving great things in the arts, business, sport and politics, but inequalities continue to exist. Girls are apparently achieving higher grades in examinations than boys, yet many women still believe that they have to work harder than men to achieve an equivalent position in the workplace. Many women blame this on career breaks, when they take time off work to bring up their babies and young children. Some people believe that sexual equality is affected by the culture in which we live which is, in turn, invariably influenced by religious beliefs. Go to www.heinemann.co.uk/hotlinks (express code 4196P) for more information on UK history; UK equality leglislation; the 2001 census.

For discussion

• How did the contraceptive pill change attitudes towards the roles of women in society?

• Why do you think sexual inequalities still exist in the workplace?

Summary

• The roles of men and women have changed over the last one hundred years.

• Equal opportunities exist for men and women both in employment and in social standing.

• There are still problems for women to overcome to reach the top of their career path and sexual equality may be affected by cultural differences.

4.2 Christian attitudes to equal rights for women

Learning outcomes

By the end of this lesson, you should be able to:

● describe Christian and biblical teachings on the roles and status of women

● explain and evaluate different views concerning the ordination of women priests

● outline Christian attitudes towards the roles of women, and explain the reasons for these attitudes

● express your own opinions on different Christian attitudes towards women.

Women and the Bible

The Bible teaches that men and women are equal: *'God created man in his own image… male and female, he created them.'* (Genesis 1:27)

Jesus treated women with great respect, even though the society he lived in at that time was dominated by men. Jesus had many female followers and he taught and helped them just as he taught and helped men. They, in turn, learned from and supported him.

A still from the film Passion of the Christ *showing Jesus on the way to his crucifixion. The woman is his mother, Mary. What is she doing?*

Activities

1 Copy the diagram below. Then look up in the Bible each of verses (from the sources given) and write down in the boxes what you think each means. What do these verses tell us about the Bible's teaching on equal rights for women?

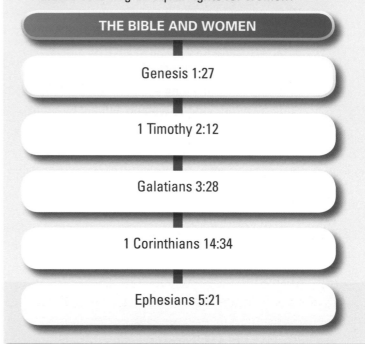

THE BIBLE AND WOMEN

Genesis 1:27

1 Timothy 2:12

Galatians 3:28

1 Corinthians 14:34

Ephesians 5:21

For discussion

● Why do you think that Jesus did not have any women among his twelve disciples?

Women as priests

Today, Christians in general consider that men and women should have equal rights, although the roles of men and women may be different. However, one serious area of inequality remains. It has only been fourteen years since women have been allowed to become priests in the Church of England – and they are still not allowed to be priests within the Roman Catholic Church. This is largely due to St Paul's teaching that: *'Women should remain silent in churches. They are not allowed to speak, but must be in submission, as the Law says'* (1 Corinthians 14:34).

Activities

2   Do you think that women are better equipped than men to be priests? Make a list of the ways in which: **(a)** women might be better than men; and **(b)** men might be better than women.

3   Write a few sentences explaining your view.

Interpreting the Bible

For Christians in the past, women were often seen as inferior because of the Biblical story of Adam and Eve. In this story, it was the woman who was sinful. Paul wrote: *'For Adam was formed first, then Eve… it was the woman who was deceived and became a sinner'* (1 Timothy 2:14).

However, the Bible was written at a time when men's themes and ideas dominated. Today, many Christians claim that they can interpret the Bible in a different way, one that does greater justice to women. For example, the story of Adam and Eve can be seen not as one about a sinful woman who tempted her husband, but as a story where the man and the woman share not only their sin and punishment, but also equally share God's love.

During Jesus's Ministry, women followers were treated very well and were far quicker to understand the identity and significance of Jesus than his male disciples were. It was the male disciples (particularly Peter and Judas) who let Jesus down in the last hours of his life; whereas the women stayed by the cross and were the first to see Jesus after his resurrection.

Yet today, there are a number of Christians (for example, evangelical Protestants) who interpret the Bible literally and argue that a woman is, first and foremost, a wife and mother and should stay at home.

Activities

4   Outline the main Christian teachings on the role and status of women.

5   **(a)** Look up in the Bible these incidents involving Jesus and women: Luke 10:38–42, Luke 13:11–13, John 20:11–18.

    (b) What do these passages suggest about Jesus's attitude towards women?

For discussion

• Do you think that Jesus would have agreed or disagreed with St Paul's teachings on the role of women?

Paul wrote: *'Wives, submit to your husbands as to the Lord. For a husband has authority over his wife just as the Christ has authority over the Church'* (Ephesians 5:21).

There is growing evidence that Christians today take a more liberal approach to the roles of men and women in the Church and society. For example, a bride no longer has to promise to obey her husband as part of the wedding service vows.

Go to www.heinemann.co.uk/hotlinks (express code 4196P) for more information on equality and human rights; UK statistics; Christianity.

Summary

• The Bible teaches that men and women are created equal.

• The teaching of St Paul seems to suggest certain inequalities.

• The Church of England has allowed the ordination of women priests since 1994, though this has been very controversial.

• Some other Churches including the Roman Catholic Church forbid the ordination of women.

 ResultsPlus
Build better answers

Explain different Christian attitudes to the role of women. (8 marks)

Basic, 0–2-mark answers
Basic answers only focus on one attitude, or they offer a variety of attitudes without explanation.

Good, 3–6-mark answers
These answers will put forward some of the differing opinions within Christianity either about the role of women in society or in the Church.

Excellent, 7–8-mark answers
The highest marks are given to answers that include a variety of opinions, identifying which types of Christians are most likely to believe the different opinions.

4.3 Muslim attitudes to equal rights for women

Learning outcomes

By the end of the lesson, you should be able to:

- describe Islamic teachings about the role of women
- explain the traditional role of women in Islam
- explain modern Islamic views on the role of women
- express your own opinions on different Islamic attitudes towards women.

Glossary

Burqa – A full-length, loose-fitting garment that only leaves the hands and feet uncovered (usually worn with a *niqab*).

Hijab – A scarf that covers the hair and shoulders.

Niqab – A veil covering the face.

Activities

For many people in Britain, clothing is thought to be the area that explains the Muslim attitude to women.

1 Look at the two women in the photo. What are the arguments for and against what each woman in the picture has chosen to wear?

Equal but different

Islam teaches that men and women are equal and created by God: '*All people are equal… as the teeth of a comb*' (Hadith).

Activities

2 Look at the spider diagram below. Write down a list of points where men and women are treated in the same way in Islam and another list of points where they are treated differently in Islam.

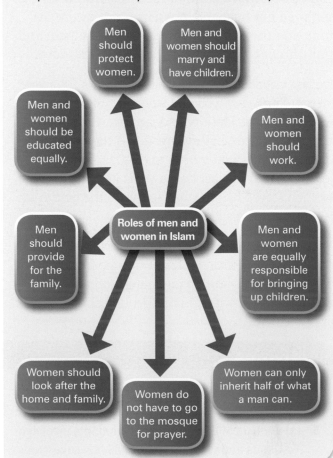

Traditionally, in Islam, men and women are seen as having different but equally important roles. The Qur'an teaches that God made men stronger and so they should protect women, who, in their turn, are required to have children.

The Qur'an stresses sexual equality strongly and every instruction given in the Qur'an applies equally to men and women: '… *for men and women who engage much in Allah's praise, for them has Allah prepared forgiveness and great reward.*' (Surah 33:35)

However, in practice this has not necessarily happened. Many modern Muslim women are seeking greater equality, claiming that the Qur'an teaches that men and women are equal in religion and education.

Clothing

The Qur'an states that both men and women should dress modestly. Men must wear loose clothing and must always be covered from the navel to the knee in public. They should not wear tight or revealing clothing.

Many Muslim women in the UK choose to wear loose-fitting Western-style dress with a headscarf or *hijab* to cover the hair and shoulders. Others may wear a *burqa* when outside the home. This is a full-length, loose fitting garment, designed so that even the outline of a woman's body cannot be seen. This is usually worn with a veil (*niqab*) to cover the face.

There is much controversy about dressing in this way. Some argue that it is outdated and that any identification of religious belief in public should be discouraged in order to maintain an equal and unprejudiced society. However, many Muslim women who wear the *niqab/burqa* or *hijab* believe that it gives them a degree of public privacy and acts as a symbol of their religious faith.

Activities

3   People in some countries believe it is wrong to wear clothes in the workplace that highlight a person's faith. Do you agree?

Worship

Unlike men, women are not obliged to attend the mosque for prayer, although many Muslim women do. In the mosque, men and women worship in separate areas to avoid distraction but they worship at the same time and follow the same imam. Girls are given the same religious education as boys in the *madrasah*. Indeed, the Hadith states: '*The search for knowledge is a duty of every Muslim, male or female.*' Women are expected to follow the Five Pillars of Islam in the same way as men.

Muslim women are free to work and many point out that the Prophet Muhammad's wife ran her own successful business. However, because a woman's first duty is to look after her children and home, she is also entitled to expect that her husband will provide for her, even if she herself is wealthy. For this reason, men are given '*a degree of advantage*' over women (Surah 2:228) because they have the responsibility of providing for the family. Go to www.heinemann.co.uk/hotlinks (express code 4196P) for more information on equality and human rights; Islam.

Activities

4   In the modern world, do you think it is right that a wealthy Muslim woman should still be provided for by her husband?

5   In your opinion, what 'degree of advantage' do men have over women?

6   In what ways have modern Islamic views changed the roles of Muslim women today?

Summary

• Traditional Islamic teaching says that men and women have different roles.

• Modern Islamic teaching suggests that men and women have equal, but different roles – the women should first and foremost care for the family, and the men should provide for them.

4.4 The UK as a multi-ethnic society

94

Learning outcomes

By the end of this lesson, you should be able to:

- explain what is meant by a multi-ethnic society
- describe the problem of racism
- describe how the UK became a multi-ethnic society
- describe some of the advantages of a multi-ethnic society
- give your opinion on the issues raised by the UK being a multi-ethnic society.

edexcel ⁝⁝ key terms

Ethnic minority – A member of an ethnic group (race) that is smaller than the majority group.

Multi-ethnic society – Where many different races and cultures live together in one society.

Racial harmony – Different races living together happily.

Racism – The belief that some races are superior to others.

The UK has a **multi-ethnic society.** This means that it is made up of many different races, cultures and nationalities living together in one society. Although today many people are worried about the numbers of different people coming to live in the UK from overseas, in fact the UK has always been a land of many races – from the Romans 2,000 years ago, through to the Saxons, the Normans and many more who have settled here. Some came to find a better life, or work, while others came to find safety from oppression.

The facts and figures

In 1991, the government carried out a census to discover how many different ethnic groups there were in the UK. Here are the main results:

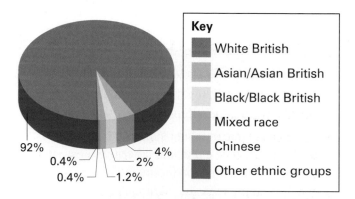

Key
- White British
- Asian/Asian British
- Black/Black British
- Mixed race
- Chinese
- Other ethnic groups

92%
0.4%
0.4%
4%
2%
1.2%

The ethnic make-up of the total population of the UK.

More recently, there has been large-scale immigration into the UK from the countries of Eastern Europe, particularly Poland. This is because these countries recently joined the European Union, giving their citizens the right to work in other European Union countries. Between 2004 and 2006, for example, there were more than 600,000 Eastern Europeans who came to live and work in the UK. Most work either in construction or in retail. There have, however, been some protests about the pressure these new immigrants have brought on housing and other public services.

In the same time period, 198,000 British citizens emigrated abroad, mostly going to live in Southern Europe, Australia or New Zealand.

However, one of the serious problems that can occur in a multi-ethnic society is **racism**. Racism is the belief that certain ethnic groups are superior to others. This has led to many people from **ethnic minorities** being persecuted and their human rights abused simply because of their nationality or the colour of their skin. For example, not many years ago there were race riots in the UK caused by unemployment and poor social conditions.

Despite these problems it is possible to live in **racial harmony** and there are many advantages to living in a multi-ethnic society:

- It helps people of different races and cultures to understand one another better.
- It gives us a wider variety of music, food, clothes and culture.
- It can bring new people with fresh ideas.

Activities

1 Look at the chart on the previous page.

   (a) What is the largest ethnic group in the UK?

   (b) What is the largest non-white group?

   (c) What do you think this tells us about multi-ethnic society in the UK?

2 Do you think it is right that citizens of the European Union should be able to work freely in other member countries? What are the advantages and disadvantages?

There are some interesting statistics on racial distribution in the UK. A government unemployment survey in 2000 found:

Unemployed	(%)
White	6
Indian	8
Afro-Caribbean	19
Bangladeshi/Pakistani	21

- Only 52 out of 3,000 top civil servants are from racial minorities.
- There were no black High Court judges.
- Only 3.3 per cent of university students were Afro-Caribbean and 10 per cent Asian.
- Black males are eight times more likely to be stopped and searched by police than white males.

Activities

3 List the disadvantages of living in a multi-ethnic society. Are they more, or less, convincing than the advantages? Say why.

4 How has living in Britain changed as a result of mass immigration?

For discussion

The photograph shows a scene from the Notting Hill Carnival.

- What does this tell us about racial harmony?
- Do you think that events such as the Notting Hill Carnival help racial harmony or hinder it? Why?

Results Plus
Exam question report

What is a multi-ethnic society? (2 marks) June 2007

How students answered

Many of the candidates who received 0 marks for this question got confused and defined 'multi-faith' instead of 'multi-ethnic' society.

Most of the candidates who scored 1 mark for this question gave the response that a multi-ethnic society is a mixture of different people.

Most candidates wrote excellent answers that explained a multi-ethnic society is one made up of different races and different cultures.

Summary

- The UK has a multi-ethnic society.
- This caused problems of racism at first. Racism still lingers today, though the situation is much better.
- Being a multi-ethnic society has many advantages, especially for understanding and appreciating different cultures and beliefs.

4.5 Government action to promote community cohesion

Learning outcomes

By the end of this lesson, you should be able to:

● explain the reasons for racism in the UK in past times

● describe some government measures to combat racism

● express your own views on the importance of racial equality and community cohesion.

edexcel ⠿ key terms

Community cohesion – A common vision and shared sense of belonging for all groups in society.

Community cohesion means different communities living together and sharing four things in common:

● a common vision and sense of belonging

● appreciating and valuing the differences between people of different cultures

● ensuring equal opportunities for all in the community

● making strong and positive relationships with people of different races.

Glossary

Racial discrimination – Treating people less favourably because of their race, colour or ethnic origin.

Racial equality – Where members of all different races are treated equally.

Racial discrimination in the UK

The UK has always offered a safe place for people from overseas. Many have come here to escape (from war, suffering or persecution), and others have come in order to get a job and make a better life for themselves and their families. This has provoked lots of different reactions from people in the UK.

For discussion

● Why do you think white people in the UK feared the rise in the number of immigrants?

● 'People should have the right to live in whatever country they wish to.' Do you agree? Give your reasons.

The reasons for prejudice among white people were:

● fear that those coming from overseas would take their jobs and their houses

● fear of the unknown – that those from overseas would change the traditional British way of life.

The result was racial discrimination, where many of the immigrants ended up:

● getting the worst paid jobs

● living in the poorest areas.

Many immigrants have encountered racial discrimination and have been treated less favourably because of their racial or ethnic origins.

Measures to combat racial discrimination

To try to prevent racial discrimination, the government passed the Race Relations Act 1976, making it unlawful to discriminate against anyone because of race, colour, ethnic or national origin in employment, housing, education or welfare services. The following were also made illegal: to stir up racial hatred; to use in public abusive or insulting words of a racial nature; or to publish articles that could stir up racism.

For discussion

Is the passing of laws the most effective way of stopping racial discrimination?

Alongside this, the government set up the Commission for Racial Equality to fight racism and to educate the public in the importance of racial equality. Today, it deals with many complaints of a racist nature. The most common ones are bullying and racism at work, for example people claiming that they are not being promoted or given better jobs because of their race.

A group of immigrant workers protesting over their poor working conditions.

Activities

1   Give a list of reasons why racial discrimination and prejudice are still problems in the UK.

2   Do you think the government's actions in recent years have been successful in preventing racism? And if so, to what extent? Give reasons for your answer.

More recently, the government has introduced a 'Britishness' test that all new immigrants to the UK must take. As well as being able to speak some English, immigrants are required to have a basic knowledge of British life. They have to answer questions such as:

- Whose statue is in the middle of Trafalgar Square?
- Who was the UK's first woman Prime Minister?
- What is the capital of Wales?

Can *you* answer these questions?

The Community Facilitation Programme and Neighbourhood Renewal Units were also set up, with the aim of ensuring that local ethnic communities would be able to:

- develop the skills needed for the world of work
- ensure that there are opportunities for young people
- provide appropriate health care
- make sure that local services meet the needs of the particular community.

Today, nearly two-thirds of ethnic minorities in the UK live in the 88 poorest areas of the country.

Go to www.heinemann.co.uk/hotlinks (express code 4196P) for more information on racial equality; community cohesion.

For discussion

- Is racism still a serious problem in the UK?
- 'Race relations in the UK are much better than in the past, though there is still a lot of work to be done.' Do you agree? Give your reasons.

Summary

- Racism in the UK in the past came from fears that immigrants would take peoples' jobs and houses.
- The government introduced measures such as the Race Relations Act to prevent discrimination.
- Today many people are encouraging communities to live and work together.

4.6 Why Christians should promote racial harmony

Learning outcomes

By the end of this lesson, you should be able to:

- explain the Bible's teaching on racial harmony
- describe the life and work of Martin Luther King
- explain the attitudes and work of Christians for racial harmony.

Christianity is opposed to racism. The Bible teaches that all races are equal in the eyes of God.

> 'For God created man in his own image.'
> (Genesis 1:27)

> 'God does not show favouritism, but accepts men from every nation.'
> (Acts 10:34–35)

> 'There is neither Jew nor Greek... you are all one in Christ.'
> (Galatians 3:29)

> 'Love your neighbour as yourself.'
> (Luke 10:27)

Jesus always treated people in the same way, no matter where they were from. For example, he healed a Roman's servant (Luke 7:1–10) and, in the Parable of the Good Samaritan, taught that people of different races and ethnic groups should not hate each other, but should follow God's command to love one another.

Activities

1 What does the following statement mean: 'God created man in his own image'?

2 What did Jesus mean by this statement: 'Love your neighbour as yourself'? Can you give a couple of real-life examples?

Martin Luther King Junior (1929–1968): a Christian who worked for racial harmony

Many Christians have been inspired by the life and work of Christian minister Dr Martin Luther King. He believed that God was on the side of the poor and the oppressed, and he dedicated his life to working for equal rights for black people in the USA, many of whom suffered oppression from white people. Dr King organised peaceful protests to persuade the government to grant equal rights to all people. In 1964 he won the Nobel Peace Prize and, thanks to his work, black people were given equal voting rights with whites in 1965.

His most famous speech was:

'I have a dream that my four little children will one day live in a nation where they will be judged not by the colour of their skin, but by the sort of people they are.'

He was assassinated by James Earl Ray in 1968.

Activities

Martin Luther King giving his famous 'I have a dream...' speech.

3 Why was the message of Martin Luther King so popular with black Americans?

4 Why did some people see him as a threat to their way of life?

5 In what ways did the message of Martin Luther King follow the teachings of Jesus Christ?

Christianity and racial harmony today

Today, Christian Churches throughout the world condemn racism and encourage all Christians to treat everyone equally.

'We affirm that racism is a direct contradiction of the gospel of Jesus.' (Methodist Church)

'Every form of social and cultural discrimination must be curbed and eradicated as incompatible with God's design.' (Catechism of the Catholic Church)

For discussion

'The Christian Church has not done enough to combat racism.' Do you agree? Give your reasons.

More recently, many Christians have been encouraged by the work of Desmond Tutu, the first black Archbishop of South Africa, who led a campaign of peaceful protests to gain equal status for black people during the time of white rule in South Africa. Although he was imprisoned several times, the peaceful campaigns he led helped to end apartheid (where black people were legally inferior to white people) in South Africa in 1994. At this time, Tutu, following the teaching of Jesus, then urged the people to forgive one another. He said:

'If it were not for faith, I am certain that lots of us would be hate-filled and bitter… but to speak of God, you must speak of your neighbour.'

In the UK, the Church of England has its own Race and Community Relations Committee, which advises Christians about issues of racism as well as advising people belonging to racial minorities on problems of unemployment and imprisonment. In a similar way, the Committee on Black Anglican Concerns helps Christian organisations to develop anti-racist programmes and gives opportunities for racial minorities to play an active role in Church.

Activities

This photograph was taken during the time of white rule in South Africa.

6   Look at the photograph.

  (a) What is the purpose behind the sign in the photograph?

  (b) How do you think it made (i) black people and (ii) white people feel? Say why.

Summary

- The Bible teaches that racism is wrong and that all people are equal.
- Many Christians have fought against racism, for example Martin Luther King and Desmond Tutu.
- The Christian Church works to encourage social harmony.

4.7 Why Muslims should promote racial harmony

Learning outcomes

By the end of this lesson, you should be able to:

- describe the Muslim worldwide community
- understand the life of Malcolm X
- describe the teachings of the Qur'an on racial harmony
- express your own opinions on these teachings and beliefs

One of the most important of all teachings in Islam is that every Muslim is part of the *ummah* – the community of Muslims worldwide, who are united by their faith irrespective of their race or colour.

Muslims all pray together in Arabic

Muslims from all over the world make the pilgrimage *(hajj)* to the holy city

How racial harmony is shown in Islam

In the month of Ramadan, all Muslims join together in times of fasting and feasting

All pray facing the *qiblah* (direction) of Makkah

This helps Muslims to understand that being a Muslim is not about race but about faith, which is beyond race or the colour of skin.

Activities

1 In what ways does the *hajj* help to improve racial awareness among Muslims?

For discussion

Do you think there will ever be true racial harmony? Give reasons for your answer.

Muslims at prayer. What clues can you get from this photo about Muslim attitudes to racial harmony?

Malcolm X (1925–1965): a famous Muslim who worked for racial equality

Malcolm X (El-Hajj Malik El-Shabazz) was an African-American Muslim who became active in campaigning for racial equality after his family was attacked by white supremacist groups.

As an adult, he became involved in drugs and petty crime and was sent to prison. There he met members of a radical Muslim religious organisation, the Nation of Islam, who taught that white society was stopping black people from achieving any power and success. The Nation of Islam was fighting for a separate state of their own with only black citizens.

Activities

The famous meeting between Malcolm X (wearing glasses) and Martin Luther King.

2 In groups, do some research into the lives and work of these two men. Present your findings to the rest of the group.

After he was freed, Malcolm joined the group and took the name 'X'. He became a minister for the Nation of Islam and spread the message through television and radio programmes.

Malcolm believed that the *hajj* was the greatest example of racial harmony, but he believed that racial harmony would be impossible in the USA unless there were some radical changes in society. *'There were tens of thousands of pilgrims from all over the world… But we were all participating in the same ritual, displaying a spirit of unity and brotherhood that my experiences in America had led to believe could not exist between the white and non-white.'*

In 1964, Malcolm X became disillusioned with the methods used by the Nation of Islam. He left the movement and founded the Muslim Mosque Inc. He campaigned for racial equality and racial brotherhood, though he feared that the way to achieve this might be through violence: *'There can be no revolution without bloodshed.'*

Malcolm X had a huge following, even though he was a very controversial figure. In 1965, when speaking at a rally, he was assassinated by three members of the Nation of Islam. His most famous speech was: *'I am not a racist. I am against every form of racism and segregation, every form of discrimination. I believe in human beings and that all human beings should be respected as such, regardless of their colour.'*

The message of the Qur'an

The revelation of the Qur'an to the Prophet was for all races and no race can claim to be better than any other: *'O humanity, I am the messenger of God to you all!'* (Surah 7:158)

In his speech during the Farewell Pilgrimage, the Prophet declared that all people were descended from Adam and Eve, and that the only thing that distinguishes one human being from another was their good or bad actions: *'People descend from Adam, and Adam was made out of dust. There is no superiority for an Arab over a non-Arab, neither for a white man over a black man…'*

Today, there are Muslims of many races, cultures and nationalities – highlighting the fact that, in Islam, all races are equal and loved by God.

For discussion

'Religion does not help racial harmony.' Do you agree? Give your reasons.

Summary

- All Muslims are united by the worldwide Islamic community – the *ummah*.
- Many Muslims have campaigned for racial harmony, for example Malcolm X.
- The Qur'an and the Prophet teach that all people are equal.

4.8 The UK as a multi-faith society

Learning outcomes

By the end of this lesson, you should be able to:

● explain what a multi-faith society is

● state some of the advantages of a multi-faith society

● state some problems that might occur within a multi-faith society

● evaluate the advantages and problems and express your own opinions.

edexcel ::: key terms

Multi-faith society – Where many different religious groups live together in one society.

Religious freedom – Where people have the right to practise their religion and change their religion.

The United Kingdom is made up of people of many different races, cultures and religions.

- is a multi-faith society.
People of different religious faiths and beliefs live alongside one another.

UK

- accepts religious pluralism.
That is, all faiths have an equal right to co-exist.

- offers religious freedom, to everyone.
That is, members of all religions are free to worship.

Before the Second World War there were few people who followed a religion other than Christianity in the UK. The first waves of large numbers of immigrants arrived after 1945, mainly from the West Indies. These were largely Christians who soon formed their own Churches. Then, in the 1960s and 1970s there was a large influx of people from India, Pakistan, Bangladesh and Hong Kong, followed later by people from Tanzania, Uganda and Kenya. This led to the growth of significant communities of Hindus, Muslims and Sikhs in the UK.

After a while, the families of these immigrants joined them. This led to the growth of religious communities and places of worship to support the new communities. Gurdwaras, mosques and temples sprang up and these became increasingly important within local communities. Although some purpose-built places of worship were put up, in the majority of cases either houses or redundant churches were converted. Today in the UK, there are around three million people who follow religions other than Christianity.

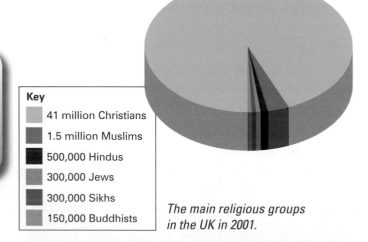

Key

☐ 41 million Christians

☐ 1.5 million Muslims

■ 500,000 Hindus

☐ 300,000 Jews

☐ 300,000 Sikhs

☐ 150,000 Buddhists

The main religious groups in the UK in 2001.

Activities

1 Draw an ideas map showing the advantages of a multi-faith society. (It might help if you think about your work on the advantages of a multi-ethnic society.) Use the diagram above to help you get started.

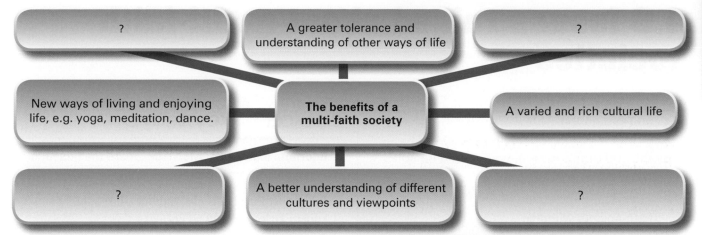

	A greater tolerance and understanding of other ways of life	?
?		
New ways of living and enjoying life, e.g. yoga, meditation, dance.	**The benefits of a multi-faith society**	A varied and rich cultural life
?	A better understanding of different cultures and viewpoints	?

Religious freedom means that religious groups from all over the world can live peacefully together. It means that people are able to understand other religions and are less worried about people who are different to themselves – a worry that has been, in the past, a major cause of racial prejudice and tension.

A demonstration by Muslims. What do you think they are protesting about?

Activities

2 In your opinion, does the UK treat members of all religions equally? List your reasons.

The challenges presented by a multi-faith society

A **multi-faith society** challenges people to think more deeply about their own faith as well as to be more open and understanding of the views of others. Hopefully, such understanding will lead to less fear and less religious persecution in the future. It has not been easy for the UK to become a multi-faith society and there is still a great deal of religious tension in certain areas. For instance, many religious believers feel that religious tolerance has led to many of their beliefs and values being ignored.

Summary

- There are many different faiths in the UK and people are free to follow whatever religion they wish.
- The advantages of a multi-faith society are that people are free to worship within the different religions, and this helps people to understand one another better.
- Some people believe that this can cause religious tension and that some religious values can be ignored.

4.9 Issues raised about multi-faith societies

Learning outcomes

By the end of this lesson, you should be able to:

- understand more about what issues a multi-faith society will face
- understand the problems of different faiths existing alongside each other
- understand some of the serious problems in the UK caused by multi-faith issues.

Most religious believers in the UK accept that people should be allowed to follow whatever religion they like. However, others are not so sure and still others say that only their own religion is right and that everyone should follow it.

There are three different viewpoints.

Religious pluralism

There are many different religions that lead to God. People should be free to follow whichever one they wish, or to follow none at all.

Inclusivism

Only one religion is completely right. The other religions, although they may lead some people to God, are not wholly right. These religions should be respected, but their followers should be encouraged to change to the 'right' faith.

Exclusivism

Only one religion is right and all the others are wrong. Members of the right faith should seek to convert all others to their faith.

Activities

1 What is a multi-faith society?
2 List some of the reasons Christians or Muslims might give for saying that *only* their religion is right.

edexcel ⠿ key terms

Interfaith marriage – Marriage where the husband and wife are from different religions.

Religious pluralism – Accepting all religions as having an equal right to co-exist.

Glossary

Conversion – Where a person changes from one religion to another.

Exclusivism – Belief that only one religion is right and all the others are wrong.

Inclusivism – Belief that one religion is completely right and the other religions have only part of the truth.

Conversion

When believers from different religions live together in one place there can be some issues if one religious group tries to convert another. If you believe your religion has the answer, and is correct, then you may feel that the right thing to do is to share this with other people but, however good the intention, this can cause conflict. The disagreement or conflict may stem from the implication that one set of beliefs is better than another, thus causing offence.

For discussion

Should members of religious faiths try to convert others to their faith?

Interfaith marriage

If two members of different religions fall in love and marry (**interfaith marriage**), it could be the beginning of a union that helps the two faith communities understand one another. In some cases it is a very positive thing. In other cases,

The bride and groom are from two different faith backgrounds. What issues might this cause in their lives together?

conflict can be caused as the families disagree on whether a couple can live together happily when the core values they hold and the beliefs they follow are different. In many religions, marrying someone outside the faith is frowned upon and even banned because marriage is regarded as the basis for bringing up children within the faith.

- Can the parents agree on how to bring up the children?
- What religion will their children belong to?
- How will their children be raised?
- Which religious festivals will they observe?
- Which religious community will the family belong to?

The mixture of beliefs and faiths can lead to confusion.

Problems arising in the UK

The multi-faith nature of society in the UK has given rise to some problems. There have been a number of violent interfaith clashes and many difficult questions have been raised.

Many people argue that the UK is still a predominantly Christian country, *not* a multi-faith one, and that Christian traditions, such as Christmas, should remain an important part of UK life.

Build better answers

Explain why trying to convert people may cause problems in a multi-faith society. (8 marks)

Basic, 0–2-mark answers
Basic answers only focus on one reason, or they offer a variety of reasons without explaining them.

Good, 3–6-mark answers
These answers offer one developed reason (or two reasons for 5–6 marks), or offer many reasons without explanations.

Excellent, 7–8-mark answers
The best answers put forward many reasons and fully explain at least two of them. The main reason that better answers use is that conversion suggests that one religion is better than another, a suggestion that is against the idea of an equal, multi-faith society.

Activities

3   Draw an ideas map of the advantages and disadvantages of multi-faith marriages.

4   'Marriages will be happiest if the couple belong to the same faith.' Do you agree? Explain why or why not.

Summary

- Different faiths existing alongside each other can raise issues although they may not cause problems.
- There are issues surrounding multi-faith marriages and the raising of children.

4.10 Ways in which religions work to promote community cohesion

106

Members of different religions do not want to live in conflict with each other. They do not want to be violent and aggressive towards each other as these actions go against all faith beliefs. However, in order to live together in harmony they will need to work together to promote community cohesion, understanding and friendship. They will have to ensure that they:

- recognise all the things that their faiths and cultures have in common
- respect the differences that arise between them
- listen to each other's views
- learn to live and work in unity rather than in opposition to each other
- share common values such as respect, tolerance, charity and non-violence.

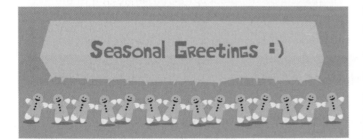

Many people now send alternatives to traditional Christmas cards.

Groups that help community cohesion

Religious groups, such as the Council of Christians and Jews and the Inter-Faith Network for the United Kingdom, have been working together in recent years to heal divisions between different faiths. They work on the basic understanding that God created all human beings to have a relationship with him. Some religious believers even suggest that all who believe in God should be united in a single faith, and that terms such as 'Christian' and 'Muslim' should no longer be used.

Religions can also promote community cohesion through the celebration of festivals and worship. In Liverpool, Church leaders hold an inaugural service in Liverpool's two cathedrals. This includes a 'walk of witness' along Hope Street, which links the two cathedrals together. Members from all world faiths take part in the service. This serves to foster unity in worship, witness and practical action.

The Muslim Council of Britain encourages Muslims in the UK to promote community cohesion by building strong communities that can give mutual support to those in need. They also urge Muslims to take an active part in UK society and not to become isolated.

The Council has also asked the police not to treat Muslim youths unfairly, and has urged the government to encourage the employment of Muslims in high-ranking jobs, for example in the police, in order to promote good Muslim role models, and also to promote a more balanced approach towards the Muslim community.

Leaders of different religions frequently meet together to discuss issues and find solutions.

For discussion

Do you think that meetings between different religious leaders help community cohesion? Explain why or why not.

Bolton Christian Community Cohesion Project

An example of a local religious organisation that is working to improve cohesion in the local community is the Bolton Christian Community Cohesion Project. Its aim is to:

'inspire and encourage Christian organisations across the borough to fulfill their potential in serving the many different communities in Bolton.'

Its work is focused on three different areas – education and youth, leisure, and the workplace. Here are some examples of its work:

- *Education and youth:* local churches, the council, police and local youth agencies provided a free family fun day for the diverse communities in East Bolton.
- *Leisure:* the project has set up a 'night cafe' that provides a safe place for people to go at night. It also addresses issues of anti-social behaviour and alcohol-related incidents.
- *Workplace:* it supports chaplaincies in hospitals, the university and town centre, which provide support to staff, students, customers, visitors and patients from the entire Bolton community, regardless of faith or the absence of faith.

Activities

4 Take each of the examples of the work done by the Bolton Christian Community Cohesion Project and explain how they may help to promote community cohesion in Bolton.

Summary

- Many national and local religious groups in the UK are working hard to establish community cohesion in the UK.
- At times problems arise and this means that religious groups have to work together and listen to each other in order to resolve the issues.

4.11 Issues of religion and community cohesion in the media

Learning outcomes

By the end of this lesson, you should be able to:

● describe how some television and radio programmes deal with religious and community cohesion issues

● describe how racism has been dealt with on television

● explain why it is important for the media to present issues sensitively and accurately.

In soap operas, programme writers often use the storyline to promote understanding or air an issue that society as a whole is grappling with at the time. These may become some of the most moving and interesting storylines in the soaps. They may include stories about racial prejudice and tension, the way a religious family comes to live within a local community without compromising their beliefs, and domestic violence towards women or the treatment of women in general.

Television documentary programmes such as *Everyman*, *Witness* and *Panorama* also devote time to important and controversial issues, for example abortion, euthanasia and race relations.

On radio, too, there are programmes on Radio 4 and one-off documentaries that deal with religious and community themes (for example, *The Moral Maze*).

Issues of religion and community cohesion are often highlighted through TV dramas and films or soaps.

Is the media biased?

One of the main problems facing the media over issues of religion and community cohesion concerns news programmes. From time to time, the news broadcasters receive complaints claiming that what they show is only one side of an argument, or that they concentrate on extremist themes giving the viewers a distorted view of what is really happening.

The first episode in The Vicar of Dibley, *'The Arrival', explores the different attitudes towards women priests through the points of view of the different characters. The community are initially divided by her arrival, however, as time goes on and they get to know her, their ideas change.*

Summary

- Many television and radio programmes deal with religious and community cohesion issues.
- There are problems concerning the presentation of some such issues on television news programmes.

Quick quiz

1 What is meant by 'discrimination'?

2 What is meant by 'ethnic harmony'?

3 How have attitudes towards gender roles in the UK changed in recent years?

4 Give two ways in which Christian and Muslim attitudes towards equal rights for women differ.

5 What is meant by 'community cohesion'?

6 What is a multi-faith society?

7 Give an example of how the government has tried to promote community cohesion.

8 Why do some Christians believe that Christianity is the only true religion?

9 What are the advantages and disadvantages of living in a multi-faith society?

10 How have religious and community issues been highlighted in television soaps?

Plenary activity

Create two characters, one male and one female. Both are in their twenties. The man is a Muslim and the woman is a Christian. They have fallen in love and decide to get married in the UK. Using some or all of the topics in this section, write a short report about the issues each character faces prior to their marriage and consider how these difficulties might be overcome.

For example, the man may be a devout Muslim and would, ideally, want his future wife to become a Muslim too. He might also want their children to grow up as Muslims. He may face opposition from his parents, who may want him to marry a Muslim girl. He must ask himself many difficult questions. Should I marry a non-Muslim? Am I right to expect my future wife to convert to Islam? What should I do if she refuses? How would it be if my children were raised as Christians?

In the same way, consider how the Christian woman feels and consider the questions she must ask herself.

Try to get into the minds of your characters, so they feel real to you and you can make them real for someone who reads your report. Try to fully understand and explain the reasons why they believe and act as they do

Student tip

When I studied these topics for my GCSE I made sure that I knew all the significant facts and understood all the main arguments for and against controversial issues. In this way, I could be sure of getting full marks for all the questions that asked for knowledge and understanding. For example, I could use my knowledge and understanding of the issues that cause racial tension to answer questions on the causes and possible solutions to such problems.

Self-evaluation checklist

Read through the following list and evaluate how well you know and understand each of the topics.
How well have you understood the topics in this section? In the first column of the table below use the following code to rate your understanding:

Green – I understand this fully

Orange – I am confident I can answer most questions on this

Red – I need to do a lot more work on this topic.

In the second and third columns you need to think about:

- Whether you have an opinion on this topic and could give reasons for that opinion if asked
- Whether you can give the opinion of someone who disagrees with you and give reasons for this alternative opinion.

Content covered	My understanding is red/orange/green	Can I give my opinion?	Can I give an alternative opinion?
How attitudes towards gender roles in the UK are changing			
Christian attitudes towards equal rights for women			
Muslim views on equal rights for women			
The UK as a multi-ethnic society			
The advantages and disadvantages of being in a multi-ethnic society			
Government legislation to prevent racism and encourage harmony			
Why Christians and Muslims should promote racial harmony			
Advantages and disadvantages of living in a multi-faith society			
Issues of conversion, interfaith marriage and raising children			
The nature of community cohesion			
Ways in which religions help to promote community cohesion			
Religious problems in the UK			
The presentation of religious issues in the media			
How the media portray issues of community cohesion			
Problems with media presentation of controversial issues			
How television and radio programmes may influence people's views about religion and community cohesion			
The question of bias in the media			

Find out more

A good way to find out more is to visit your local community centre, college or library and find out what multi-faith or multi-ethnic events are taking place in your area. For example, there may be a carnival, or a local religious or ethnic group may be celebrating an important festival in a nearby park. Take the opportunity to pick up information leaflets that will tell you what is going on and what the events are all about. And don't forget to look in the local newspaper or listen to local radio and television to find out what is going on in your area.

exam**zone**

Know Zone
Religion and community cohesion

Introduction

In the exam you will see a choice of two questions on this section. Each question will include four tasks, which test your knowledge, understanding and evaluation of the material covered. A 2-mark question will ask you to define a term; a 4-mark question will ask your opinion on a point of view; an 8-mark question will ask you to explain a particular belief or idea; a 6-mark question will ask for your opinion on a point of view and ask you to consider an alternative point of view.

Mini exam paper

(a) What is a **multi-ethnic society?** (2 marks)

> Just give a short, accurate definition.

(b) Do you think that women should have equal rights in religion?

Give **two** reasons for your point of view. (4 marks)

> You must give two clear and properly thought-out reasons – ones you have learned in class. Always use good English and avoid terms such as 'rubbish' or 'stupid' as these don't show that you are able to think things through carefully.

(c) Explain why mixed-faith marriages can cause problems for religious families. (8 marks)

> The word 'explain' means you should give details of the problems that **religious families** may have to deal with when faced with the issue of a mixed-faith marriage. Remember as well that you are writing about the problems of a religious family, so these problems will be of a **religious** nature. Don't just **list** them – explain **why** they are problems. This question is worth 8 marks so spend a longer time on it. You will also be assessed on your use of language in this question.

(d) 'If everyone were **religious** there would be no racism.' In your answer you should refer to at least one religion.

(i) Do you agree? Give reasons for your opinion. (3 marks)

> In your answer you should state whether or not you agree with the statement. You should also give reasons for your opinion.

(ii) Give reasons why some people may disagree with you. (3 marks)

> Now you must give the **opposite** point of view. As before, use reasons you have learned in class. You must show you understand why people have these other views, even if you don't agree with them.

Mark scheme

(a) You can earn **2 marks** for a correct answer, and **1 mark** for a partially correct answer.

(b) To earn up to the full **4 marks** you need to give two reasons and develop them fully. Two brief reasons or only one without any development will earn **2 marks**.

(c) You can earn **7–8 marks** by giving up to four reasons, but the fewer reasons you give, the more you must develop them. Because you are being assessed on use of language, you also need to take care to express your understanding in a clear style of English, and make some use of specialist vocabulary.

(d) To go beyond **3 marks** for the whole of this question you must refer to at least one religion. The more you are able to develop your reasons the more marks you will earn. Three simple reasons can earn you the same mark as one fully developed reason.

Results Plus

Maximise your marks

(c) Explain why mixed-faith marriages may cause problems for religious families. (8 marks)

Student answer	Examiner comments	Improved student answer
Mixed-faith marriages cause problems to religious families because the family may feel that their religion is right and the other religion is wrong.	The candidate has given a reason but this has not been developed fully. Develop this reason to explain why this is a problem.	Mixed-faith marriages may cause problems for religious families because members will have different beliefs and values. For example, the couple will need to agree on how to bring up their children, and what religion their children will belong to. There could be controversy over key issues such as homosexuality and arranged marriages.
Also, they may feel that if their son or daughter is getting married, that they will have to change their religious faith and join a religion whose teachings they do not believe in.	Again, a good reason is given but this is not developed. To gain top marks candidates need to say more about why mixed-faith marriage causes problems, not just what the problems are.	If one of the two people getting married decides to practise a different religion to suit their partner's family, this might cause worry and concern. For example, family members might worry that practising a religion that they haven't grown up with would be against the will of God, if the belief is not genuine.
Finally, the couple may not be able to have a religious wedding because of their different faiths and this means the family will not be able to celebrate the wedding properly.	This is another good reason which has not been developed. This answer will gain 4 marks, because the candidate has given some good reasons, but they have not really developed their answer. Using a good example can be very effective. In this case you could use an example as follows: if a Muslim and a Christian married and the children grew up as Muslims, the Christian grandparents may worry, for example, about whether or not the children could receive Christmas presents.	The couple may not be able to have a religious wedding because of their different faiths and this means the family will not be able to celebrate the union according to the traditions they believe in. Also, if a Muslim and Christian marry, for example, the Christian side of the family may worry about whether they should give Christmas gifts or not, and both sides could worry about how to deal with religious festivals.

Zone In!

Have you ever become so absorbed in a task that suddenly it feels entirely natural and easy to perform? This is a feeling familiar to many athletes and performers. They work hard to recreate it in competition in order to do their very best. It's a feeling of being 'in the zone', and if you can achieve that same feeling in an examination, the chances are you'll perform brilliantly.

The good news is that you can get 'in the zone' by taking some simple steps in advance of the exam. Here are our top tips.

UNDERSTAND IT

Make sure you understand the exam process and what revision you need to do. This will give you confidence and also help you to get things into proportion. These pages are a good place to find some starting pointers for performing well in exams.

FRIENDS AND FAMILY

Make sure that your friends and family know when you want to revise. Even share your revision plan with them. Learn to control your times with them, so you don't get distracted. This means you can have better quality time with them when you aren't revising, because you aren't worrying about what you ought to be doing.

DEAL WITH DISTRACTIONS

Think about the issues in your life that may interfere with revision. Write them all down. Then think about how you can deal with each so they don't affect your revision.

COMPARTMENTALISE

You might not be able to deal with all the issues that can distract you. For example, you may be worried about a friend who is ill, or just be afraid of the exam. In this case, there is still a useful technique you can use. Put all of these worries into an imagined box in your mind at the start of your revision (or in the exam) and mentally lock it. Only open it again at the end of your revision session (or exam).

DIET AND EXERCISE

Make sure you eat sensibly and exercise as well! If your body is not in the right state, how can your mind be? A substantial breakfast will set you up for the day, and a light evening meal will keep your energy levels high.

BUILD CONFIDENCE

Use your revision time not only to revise content, but also to build your confidence in readiness for tackling the examination. For example, try tackling a short sequence of easy tasks in record time.

 More on the CD

Planning Zone

The key to success in exams and revision often lies in good planning. Knowing **what** you need to do and **when** you need to do it is your best path to a stress-free experience. Here are some top tips in creating a great personal revision plan.

First of all, *know your strengths and weaknesses.*

Go through each topic making a list of how well you think you know the topic. Use your mock examination results and/or any other test results that are available as a check on your self-assessment. This will help you to plan your personal revision effectively, putting extra time into your weaker areas.

Next, *create your plan!*

Remember to make time for considering how topics interrelate.

For example, in PE you will be expected to know not just about the various muscles, but how these relate to various body types.

The specification quite clearly states when you are expected to be able to link one topic to another so plan this into your revision sessions.

You will be tested on this in the exam and you can gain valuable marks by showing your ability to do this.

Finally, *follow the plan!*

You can use the revision sections in the following pages to kick-start your revision.

MAY

SUNDAY	MONDAY	TUES
30	30	1
		view Secti
		complete t
		ractice ex
		question

Be realistic about how much time you can devote to your revision, but also make sure you put in enough time. Give yourself regular breaks or different activities to give your life some variance. Revision need not be a prison sentence!

Find out your exam dates. Go to the Edexcel website **www.edexcel.com** to find all final exam dates, and check with your teacher.

Chunk your revision in each subject down into smaller sections. This will make it more manageable and less daunting.

Draw up a list of all the dates from the start of your revision right through to your exams.

13

Review Sectio
Complete three
practice exam

20

Review Sectio
Try the Keywor
Quiz again

Make sure you allow time for assessing your progress against your initial self-assessment. Measuring progress will allow you to see and be encouraged by your improvement. These little victories will build your confidence.

22

EXAM DAY!

27

28

29

Know Zone
Section 1: Believing in God

In this section, you need to show the examiner not only that you know about issues relating to belief in God (AO1), but that you understand why Christians differ in the beliefs they hold (AO2).

This is an important skill to demonstrate, but not an easy one. It means that you have to have learned the facts first – for example, what it means to say that God is omni-benevolent – and then you have to consider why this may lead to different beliefs among Christians. Some may believe this means we should expect God to perform miracles, while others may believe it means God should answer prayer. Other Christians may argue that God doesn't *have* to do either of these things, but that when he doesn't people should not think this means he isn't loving.

Christians have different approaches to solving the problem of evil: God's loving and powerful nature suggests that he wouldn't allow evil to occur – and yet we can't deny that it does.

You need to show you understand why it is that Christians can have differing beliefs and yet all still be genuinely Christian.

As part of the AO2 assessment you also have to be able to explain your own views and assess why and how they differ from other possible views. The issue here is that you can be critical of your own views as well as those of others and recognise the variety of beliefs that can be held.

Revision

Look back at the KnowZone that appears at the end of the section, on pages 26–29. Read through the Self-evaluation checklist and think about which are your stronger and weaker areas, so that you can focus on the ones you are less confident about. You may like to try the Quick quiz again, the Plenary activity, or the Support activity below.

When you are ready for some exam practice, read through the KnowZone on pages 28–29. Then you might like to attempt the questions on the right.

Support activity

Question (d) below about religious broadcasting on television needs to be based on real evidence of television programmes on religious themes, so make sure you have some at hand to refer to. Pick any suitable programme and watch it as part of your revision. Jot down some notes either while you are watching or just after. You may like to consider these quotes and whether the programme supports or does not support the views:

'Religious programmes on television are usually supportive of religious believers'

'Religious programmes on television say more about reasons not to believe in God than to believe in him'

'Television programmes about religious beliefs discourage people from believing in God'.

Practice exam questions

(a) What is meant by **numinous**? (2 marks)

(b) Do you think God is the cause of the universe?

Give **two** reasons for your point of view. (4 marks)

(c) Choose **one** religion and explain how its followers respond to the problem of evil and suffering. (8 marks)

(d) 'Religious programmes on television or the radio encourage you to believe in God.' In your answer you should refer to at least one religion.

(i) Do you agree? Give reasons for your opinion. (3 marks)

(ii) Give reasons why some people may disagree with you. (3 marks)

The material in this section tends to deal with issues that are not just of concern to religious people, but to everyone. We all care about matters of life and death, not least because we will all die! But, until we do, we want to be sure that our life and the lives of others, whether they are close to us or not, are treated with respect.

In this section, it is important that you ensure you gain marks from considering the particular concerns of religious believers even though they may be quite different from your own. Some of these concerns may also be shared by some non-religious believers. Make sure you understand what makes these views distinctive for religious believers. For example, issues such as the sanctity of life and the belief that God created human beings for a special purpose are likely to form part of the religious position on matters of life and death. So, a religious believer might say this is the reason they are against euthanasia; but a non-religious person might also be against it, because they think it is always more important to preserve life than take it away.

Revision

Look back at the KnowZone that appears at the end of the section, on pages 54–57. Read through the Self-evaluation checklist and think about which are your stronger and weaker areas, so that you can focus on the ones you are less confident about. You may like to try the Quick quiz again, the Plenary activity, or the Support activity below.

When you are ready for some exam practice, read through the KnowZone on pages 56–57. Then you might like to attempt the questions on the right.

Support activity

Question (d) below is about the paranormal. It is probably one of the trickier questions you can get, as it really is a matter of opinion. No one can actually prove whether paranormal activity is genuine or not. Your understanding of this area would be helped by finding out, as a class or in small groups, about some popular views on the paranormal. Find out about television shows and so-called 'celebrity' mediums such as Tony Stockwell. They have an enormous following. Discuss why you think this is the case, and if that in any way proves they are genuinely in touch with the paranormal.

Practice exam questions

(a) What is **resurrection**? (2 marks)

(b) Do you agree with abortion?
Give **two** reasons for your point of view. (4 marks)

(c) Choose **one religion other than Christianity** and explain why most of the followers of that religion are against euthanasia. (8 marks)

(d) 'The paranormal proves that there is life after death.' In your answer you should refer to at least one religion.
(i) Do you agree? Give reasons for your opinion. (3 marks)
(ii) Give reasons why some people may disagree with you. (3 marks)

Know Zone
Section 3: Marriage and the family

Obtaining good AO2 answers in this section depends on your being able to distinguish between genuine difference of opinion on the one hand and prejudice or ignorance on the other.

For example, although religious believers may have a range of views on homosexuality, those views will be supported by what they hold to be a genuine interpretation of sacred texts or other valid religious teachings. Even if you don't agree with them, in most cases they will be held for good reasons, not just out of prejudice for or against homosexual people. Remember, too, not to assume that all religious people are against everything! Many religious believers today adopt a liberal approach to a lot of these issues, and you need to show that you understand why that is the case.

Revision

Look back at the KnowZone that appears at the end of the section, on pages 82–85. Read through the Self-evaluation checklist and think about which are your stronger and weaker areas, so that you can focus on the ones you are less confident about. You may like to try the Quick quiz again, the Plenary activity, or the Support activity below.

When you are ready for some exam practice, read through the KnowZone on pages 84–85. Then you might like to attempt the questions on the right.

Support activity

Question (b) on contraception asks for your opinion without specifying that you refer to religion. It is a question that need not have anything to do with religion, but at the same time you need to show that you do understand religious views and that they might be held for special reasons. As a group or in pairs compare the attitudes towards contraception shown in the two contrasting websites. For pregnancy advice and contraception, these can be accessed on our hotlinks website, www.heinemann.co.uk/hotlinks (express code 4196P).

What do they tell you about how believers and non-believers feel about contraception? What audiences do you think they are aimed at? Are they persuasive websites? (This means: do they convey their messages in a way that would encourage people to adopt their views?)

Practice exam questions

(a) What is **remarriage?** (2 marks)

(b) Do you think it is right to use contraception?

   Give **two** reasons for your point of view. (4 marks)

(c) Explain why some Christians allow divorce and some do not. (8 marks)

(d) 'Family life is more important for religious people than for non-religious people.' In your answer you should refer to at least one religion.

   (i) Do you agree? Give reasons for your opinion. (3 marks)

   (ii) Give reasons why some people may disagree with you. (3 marks)

Know Zone
Section 4: Religion and community cohesion

Similarly to matters of life and death, the issues you study in community cohesion are ones of general concern, not just of concern to religious believers. Your task in the exam is to show that you understand both how religious believers tackle these issues and the beliefs that underlie their attitudes to matters of community cohesion.

These issues are important for society as well as for religion, but you need to distinguish between these in the exam. For example, a question that asks you if you agree that there should be equal rights for women in religion demands a different response from you than if the question asked whether women should have equal rights in society.

In question (d) in this section, make sure that you do not express any personal feelings that may appear to be unsympathetic to community cohesion. This is not an appropriate response for an examination, where you need to deal with matters in an academic way.

Revision

Look back at the KnowZone that appears at the end of the section, on pages 110–113. Read through the Self-evaluation checklist and think about which are your stronger and weaker areas, so that you can focus on the ones you are less confident about. You may like to try the Quick quiz again, the Plenary activity, or the Support activity below.

When you are ready for some exam practice, read through the KnowZone on pages 112–113. Then you might like to attempt the questions on the right.

Support activity

To help you answer question (b) about whether religious believers have the right to convert you, discuss as a group any experience you have had of either trying to convert others to your faith or when someone tried to convert you. Listen carefully to each other's views and don't make any judgements. Instead, after you've shared any experiences of this, make a list of the feelings that you think people from each group may have had. For example, feelings of rejection, anger and bewilderment may all be relevant, but also feelings of encouragement, well-being or comfort.

Practice exam questions

(a) What is **racism**? (2 marks)

(b) Do people from a different religion have the right to try to convert you?

Give **two** reasons for your point of view. (4 marks)

(c) Choose **one religion other than Christianity**, and explain why the followers of that religion should help to promote racial harmony. (8 marks)

(d) 'Women should have the same rights as men in religion.' In your answer you should refer to at least one religion.

(i) Do you agree? Give reasons for your opinion. (3 marks)

(ii) Give reasons why some people may disagree with you. (3 marks)

Don't Panic Zone

As you get close to completing your revision, the Big Day will be getting nearer and nearer. Many students find this the most stressful time and tend to go into panic mode, either working long hours without really giving their brains a chance to absorb information. or giving up and staring blankly at the wall.

Panicking simply makes your brain seize up and you find that information and thoughts simply cannot flow naturally. You become distracted and anxious, and things seem worse than they are. Many students build the exams up into more than they are. Remember: the exams are not trying to catch you out! If you have studied the course, there will be no surprises on the exam paper!

Student tip

I know how silly it is to panic, especially if you've done the work and know your stuff. I was asked by a teacher to produce a report on a project I'd done, and I panicked so much I spent the whole afternoon crying and worrying. I asked other people for help, but they were panicking too. In the end, I calmed down and looked at the task again. It turned out to be quite straightforward and, in the end, I got my report finished first and it was the best of them all!

In the exam you don't have much time, so you can't waste it by panicking. The best way to control panic is simply to do what you have to do. Think carefully for a few minutes, then start writing and as you do, the panic will drain away.

Don't panic

Exam Zone

You will have one and a half hours for this exam paper and in that time you have to answer **four** questions, one on each of the four sections you have studied: Beliefs about God, Matters of life and death, Marriage and family and Community cohesion.

In each section, you can make a choice from two questions.

Each question will be made up of four different parts.

- A 2-mark question will ask you to define a term
- a 4-mark question will ask your opinion on a point of view
- an 8-mark question will ask you to explain a particular belief or idea
- a 6-mark question will ask for your opinion on a point of view and ask you to consider an alternative point of view.

Effectively you shouldn't spend more than 22.5 minutes on each section (that's 90 minutes divided by 4):

- the 8-mark question deserves the most attention, so that's around 9 minutes
- the 2-mark question should take you 1.5 minutes, then
- 5 minutes for the 4-mark question, and
- the remaining 7 minutes for the 6-mark question.

Obviously you can give or take here or there, and your teacher may guide you differently, but as long as you don't go over 22.5 minutes altogether and the length of each of your answers is appropriate for the number of marks available, then you'll be on the right lines.

Meet the exam paper

This diagram shows the front cover of the exam paper. These instructions, information and advice will always appear on the front of the paper. It is worth reading it carefully now. Check you understand it. Now is a good opportunity to ask your teacher about anything you are not sure of here.

Print your surname here, and your other names afterwards to ensure that the exam board awards the marks to the right candidate.

Here you fill in the school's exam number.

Ensure that you understand exactly how long the examination will last, and plan your time accordingly.

Note that the quality of your written communication will also be marked. Take particular care to present your thoughts and work at the highest standard you can, for maximum marks.

Here you fill in your personal exam number. Take care when writing it down because the number is important to the exam board when writing your score.

In this box, the examiner will write the total marks you have achieved in the exam paper.

Make sure that you understand exactly which questions from which sections you should attempt.

Don't feel that you have to fill the answer space provided. Everybody's handwriting varies, so a long answer from you may take up as much space as a short answer from someone else.

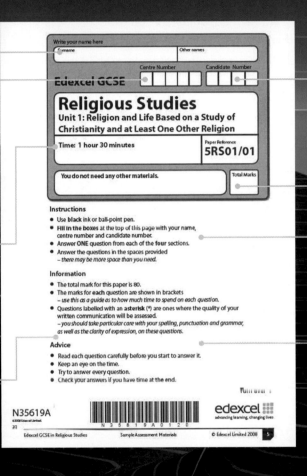

Understanding the language of the exam paper

Describe	The examiner is looking for a concise and organised account. Jot down three or four points in the margin that you want to include in your answer. Arrange them in the most logical order.
Explain how	The examiner is trying to discover whether you know what a believer thinks, and why they think that. The more detail you can give, the more marks you will receive.
Give reasons for your answer	You need to provide an explanation.
Do you agree?	You are free to agree or disagree. What makes a difference is how well you back up your case.

Zone out

This section provides answers to the most common questions students have about what happens after they complete their exams. For more information, visit www.heinemann.co.uk/hotlinks (express code 4196P) and click on examzone.

About your grades

Whether you've done better than, worse than, or just as you expected, your grades are the final measure of your performance on your course and in the exams. On this page we explain some of the information that appears on your results slip and tell you what to do if you think something is wrong. We answer the most popular questions about grades and look at some of the options facing you.

When will my results be published?

Results for summer examinations are issued on the **middle** two Thursdays in August, with GCE first and GCSE second. November exam results are issued in January, January exam results are issued in March and March exam results are issued in April.

Can I get my results online?

Visit www.heinemann.co.uk/hotlinks (express code 4196P) and click on Results Plus, where you will find detailed student results information including the 'Edexcel Gradeometer' which demonstrates how close you were to the nearest grade boundary.

I haven't done as well as I expected. What can I do now?

First of all, talk to your subject teacher. After all the teaching, tests and internal examinations that you have had, he/she is the person who best knows what grade you are capable of achieving. Take your results slip to your subject teacher, and go through the information on it in detail. If you both think there is something wrong with the result, the school or college can apply to see your completed examination paper and then, if necessary, ask for a re-mark immediately. The original mark can be confirmed or lowered, as well as raised, as a result of a re-mark.

How do my grades compare with those of everybody else who sat this exam?

You can compare your results with those of others in the UK who have completed the same examination using the information on the Edexcel website accessed at www.heinemann.co.uk/hotlinks (express code 4196P) by clicking on Edexcel.

I achieved a higher mark for the same unit last time. Can I use that result?

Yes. The higher score is the one that goes towards your overall grade. Even if you sat a unit more than twice, the best result will be used automatically when the overall grade is calculated. You do not need to ask the exam board to take into account a previous result. This will be done automatically so you can be assured that all your best unit results have gone into calculating your overall grade.

What happens if I was ill over the period of my examinations?

If you become ill before or during the examination period you are eligible for special consideration. This also applies if you have been affected by an accident, bereavement or serious disturbance during an examination.

If my school has requested special consideration for me, is this shown on my Statement of Results?

If your school has requested special consideration for you, it is not shown on your results slip, but it will be shown on a subject mark report that is sent to your school or college. If you want to know whether special consideration was requested for you, you should ask your Examinations Officer.

Can I have a re-mark of my examination paper?

Yes, this is possible, but remember that only your school or college can apply for a re-mark, not you or your parents/carers. First of all, you should consider carefully whether or not to ask your school or college to make a request for a re-mark. It is worth knowing that very few re-marks result in a change to a grade – not because Edexcel is embarrassed that a change of marks has been made, but simply because a re-mark request has shown that the original marking was accurate. Check the closing date for re-marking requests with your Examinations Officer.

When I asked for a re-mark of my paper, my subject grade went down. What can I do?

There is no guarantee that your grades will go up if your papers are re-marked. They can also go down or stay the same. After a re-mark, the only way to improve your grade is to take the examination again. Your school or college Examinations Officer can tell you when you can do that.

How many times can I re-sit a unit?

You may re-sit a modular GCSE Science or Mathematics module test once, prior to taking your terminal examination and before obtaining your final overall grade. The highest score obtained on either the first attempt or the re-sit counts towards your final grade. If you enter a module in GCSE Mathematics at a different tier, this does not count as a re-sit. If you are on the full modular Religious Studies GCSE course, and sat the first unit last year, you may re-sit module 1 when you sit module 2 to maximise your full course grade.

For much more information, go to www.heinemann.co.uk/hotlinks (express code 4196P) and click on examzone.

Glossary

This is an extended glossary containing definitions that will help you in your studies. Edexcel key terms are not included as all of these are defined in the lessons themselves.

Akhirah – Life after death.

al'Jannah – Heaven.

Analogy – A way of comparing two similar things to highlight their similarities.

Annulment – A declaration by the Church that a marriage never lawfully took place.

Apartheid – Where black people are treated as legally inferior to white people.

Baptism – The Christian rite of **initiation** that welcomes a person into the Christian community.

Barzakh – In Islam, the barrier preventing unbelievers, after death, from returning to the earth to accomplish the good they have left undone.

Bible – The sacred text of Christianity.

'Big Bang' theory – The theory that an enormous explosion started the universe around 15 billion years ago.

Burqa – A full-length, loose-fitting garment that only leaves the hands and feet uncovered (usually worn with a *niqab*).

Catechism – An elementary manual of Christian doctrine.

Causation – The principle that everything is caused by something else.

Celibacy – Refraining from sexual activity for religious reasons.

Church school – School that educates children within a Christian environment.

Communion of saints – The belief that Christians will live on after death and that living Christians can share with those who have died.

Confession of sins – Admitting wrongdoing against God.

Confirmation – Where a young Christian makes the **baptism** vows for him- or herself.

Conversion – Where a person changes from one religion to another.

Covenant – Literally, an agreement between two parties.

Creed – Summary statement of religious beliefs, often recited in **worship**.

Creationists – Religious believers who believe that the world was created by God in six days, exactly as described in Genesis.

Darar – Islamic principle of injury, which demands that no one should be hurt or cause hurt to others.

Design – The appearance of order and purpose.

Divorce – The legal termination of a **marriage**.

Ensoulment – The Muslim belief that a life begins once the soul has entered the **foetus**.

Equality – The state of everyone having equal rights regardless of their gender, race or class.

Ethnic – Relating to a group of people having a common national or cultural tradition.

Eucharist – A Christian service commemorating the death and resurrection of Jesus Christ, in which bread and wine are consumed.

Evolution – The gradual development of species over millions of years.

Exclusivism – Belief that only one religion is right and all the others are wrong.

Extended family – Parents, children and other relations, all living together.

Extra-marital sex – Sex that takes place outside, or before, **marriage**.

Faith – Belief in something without total proof.

Foetus – An unborn baby at least eight weeks old.

Hadith – The sayings of the Prophet.

Hajj – Annual pilgrimage to **Makkah**, which each Muslim must undertake at least once in a lifetime if he or she has the health and wealth.

Halal – That which is permitted or lawful in Islam.

Haram – That which is forbidden or unlawful in Islam.

Heaven – A place of paradise where God rules.

Hell – A place of horrors where Satan rules.

Hifdh ad-din – The preservation of religion.

Hijab – A scarf which covers the hair and shoulders.

Holiness – Having the characteristic of being set apart for God's purposes.

Holocaust – Destruction or murder on a mass scale, especially that of Jews under the German Nazi regime in the Second World War.

Holy Spirit – God as spiritually active in the world.

Hospice – A type of hospital where the terminally ill are cared for and prepared for death.

Iddah – The waiting period following a statement of **divorce**, to ensure that no child is expected and to offer the chance of reconciliation.

Imam – A person who leads prayers in a **mosque**.

Inclusivism – Belief that one religion is completely right and the other religions have only part of the truth.

Initiation ceremony – A ritual, such as **baptism**, which welcomes a person as a new member of a community or group that holds a certain set of beliefs.

Intercession – Praying for others.

Jahannam – Hell.

Judgement – The act of judging people and their actions.

Liturgy – Service of **worship** according to a prescribed ritual.

Madrasah – An Islamic school for both children and adults, where the basis of education is learning and understanding the **Qur'an**.

Maqasid ash-Sharia'ah – The preservation of life.

Makkah (Mecca) – The birthplace of the Prophet Muhammad.

Marriage – The legal union of a man and a woman.

Meditation – Thinking deeply about spiritual things.

Methodism – A branch of Christianity that came into existence through the work of John Wesley in the 18th century.

Mosque – A Muslim place of **worship**.

Mystical experience – Experiencing God's voice or a religious vision.

Natural selection – The way in which species naturally select the best characteristics for survival.

Near-death experience – An experience after clinical death and before resuscitation.

Niqab – A veil covering the face.

Nuclear family – Two parents (a man and a woman) living together with their children.

Paranormal – Unexplained things that are thought to have spiritual causes, e.g. ghosts.

Petitions – Requests made of God.

Polygamy – Legally being married to more than one spouse.

Priest – Specially called/chosen person who is ordained to be a minister of the **sacraments**.

Protestant – That part of the Christian Church that became distinct from the **Roman Catholic** and other churches, when their members 'protested' the centrality of the Bible and other beliefs.

Purgatory – Roman Catholic belief in a place where those who do not go straight to **Heaven** go into a state of waiting and preparation for Heaven where their souls will be cleansed.

Qur'an – The sacred book of Islam.

Racial discrimination – Treating people less favourably because of their race, colour or ethnic origin.

Racial equality – Where members of all different races are treated equally.

Reconstituted family – Where two sets of children (stepbrothers and sisters) become one family when their divorced parents marry each other.

Roman Catholic – That part of the Christian Church owing loyalty to the Pope in Rome.

Sacrament – An outward sign of an inward blessing, as in **baptism** or the **Eucharist**.

Seance – A meeting at which people attempt to contact the dead.

Shari'ah law – Law based on the **Qur'an**, the teachings of Muhammad and the work of Islamic scholars.

Shi'ah school – Muslims who believe that only the caliph Ali was rightly guided.

Surah – A division of the **Qur'an**.

Testimony – A public statement of **faith** and belief.

Thanksgiving – Giving thanks to God for what he has done.

Theist – A person who believes in God.

Tongues – The gift, from the **Holy Spirit**, of praying/speaking in unknown languages.

Ummah – The worldwide family of Islam.

Worship – Praising God.

zakah – The tax that Muslims pay for the poor.

Index

In the following index, Edexcel key terms are given in **bold** and the first page number, also in bold, will lead you to the definition. For further definitions of unfamiliar words, see also the Glossary on pages 124–5

Edexcel GCSE Religious Studies Unit 1A
Religion and Life
Christianity & Islam

Gordon Reid • Sarah Tyler

Edexcel GCSE Religious Studies Unit 1A Religion and Life: Christianity & Islam is tailored to the 2009 Edexcel GCSE Religious Studies specification. Written by experienced Edexcel examiners and teachers, it provides all the subject content and exam practice needed for success.

- *Learning outcomes* provide a clear overview of what students will learn
- *Edexcel key terms* are highlighted and defined for easy reference and *fascinating facts* give learning depth and relevance
- *Activities* support and embed understanding
- *For discussion* topics provide the opportunity for debate.

Combining real exam performance data with examiner insight to give guidance on how to **achieve better results**.

exam zone A dedicated suite of revision resources for **complete exam success**.

Also available from Edexcel
Unit 2A: Religion and Life: Christianity
978 1 846904 20 2
Unit 3A: Religion and Life: Catholic Christianity
978 1 846904 21 9
Unit 4A: Religion and Life: Islam
978 1 846904 22 6
Unit 8B: Religion and Society: Christianity & Islam
978 1 846904 23 3
Unit 9C: Christianity
978 1 846904 24 0
Unit 10C: Catholic Christianity
978 1 846904 25 7
Unit 11C: Islam
978 1 846904 26 4
Unit 16D: Mark's Gospel
978 1 846904 27 1

Each book covers one unit - the content for a short-course GCSE Edexcel Religious Studies qualification. For a full course students need to take two units.
To find out more about the other titles in the Edexcel GCSE Religious Studies series go to: www.edexcel.com/gcse

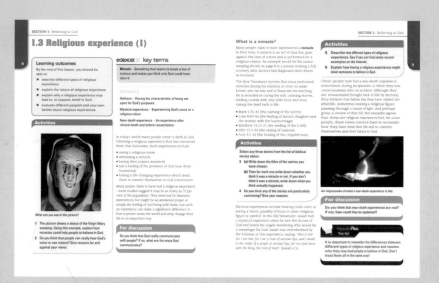

Active Teach Enlarge and project every part and every page of the Student Book for focused whole-class teaching